The

LOU CONTER STORY

From USS Arizona Survivor to Unsung American Hero

Louis A. Conter,
Annette C. Hull, and Warren R. Hull

The Lou Conter Story: From USS Arizona Survivor to Unsung American Hero

Published by Wheatmark®
2030 East Speedway Boulevard, Suite 106
Tucson, Arizona 85719 USA
www.wheatmark.com

ISBN: 978-1-62787-859-3 (paperback)
ISBN: 978-1-62787-860-9 (ebook)
LCCN: 2020925420

Bulk ordering discounts are available through Wheatmark, Inc. For more information, email orders@wheatmark.com or call 1-888-934-0888.

Contents

FOREWORD

by Ed Bonner

I FIRST MET LOU Conter at an Eagle Scout Court of Honor in 2013. I was the elected sheriff-coroner-marshal of Placer County, California, at the time, and Lou and I were participating in awarding the Boy Scouts of America's highest honor, Eagle Scout, to a young man. Here I was, sharing the stage with a survivor of the USS *Arizona*. I am a history fan and an unabashed admirer of a group of people commonly known as the Greatest Generation. Needless to say, I was starstruck. After the ceremony and before the assembled guests had departed, I formally reintroduced myself to Lou and his wife, Val. I stumbled to find the words to express my appreciation and excitement to meet him. I think I must have amused Val, and she asked me to stop by their house anytime for a cup of coffee. The next week, I did just that and visited the couple in their home in the adjacent county many times. Val was one of the most gracious people I have ever had the pleasure to share time with. Even though she had serious health issues, she would make coffee, and the three of us would gather at their kitchen table and talk. I had seen a photo of the USS *Arizona* and memorial at the World War II Valor in the Pacific National Monument taken from above the wreckage in an issue of the *National Geographic* that was dedicated to our national parks. There was a quote from President George H. W. Bush at the fiftieth remembrance of the attack on Pearl Harbor; "Today we honor those who gave their lives at this place, half a century ago . . . Think of how it was for these heroes of the Harbor, men who were also husbands, fathers, brothers, sons. Imagine the chaos of the guns and smoke, flaming water, and ghastly carnage. Two thousand, four hundred and three Americans gave their lives. But in this haunting place, they live forever in our memory, reminding us gently, selflessly, like chimes in the distant night." Lou Conter was in the audience that day. It was the first of many such remembrances he would travel to. There I was, visiting with a man who was telling me firsthand the events that had transpired that morning and the days that followed. As I listened in awe, I was aware that I was being walked through a significant piece of American history. One of my first lessons— and one Lou would often repeat—was that December 7, 1941, was only one day in years of war and conflict. It was one day in the life of this American sailor—one day in the life of this man. I'm sure my jaw must have dropped as he told me of his life before Pearl Harbor and after. In my mind, Lou Conter was the most interesting man in the world! I would leave his company and write down the things he had told me in order to help me remember, try to process the information he had shared, and put it into perspective.

When Lou would give a talk in public, he always referred to it as a briefing. He graciously stopped by my office and gave a briefing to my command staff. He consented to be our honored keynote speaker at the Placer Law Enforcement Agencies Honors and Awards Ceremony. This was an annual event for all public safety organizations doing business in the jurisdiction. City, county, state, and federal partners sat in respectful silence as he delivered his remarks about fate, service, sacrifice, and courage.

He had supplied me with documents and photos that would be used in a presentation about his background.

I was honored to attend many briefings with Lou and continued to learn more.

Lou Conter was born on September 13, 1921, and attended Wheatridge High School in Wheatridge, Colorado.

He joined the US Navy in 1939 and was recognized by his superiors as a studious young man, earning the rank of quartermaster third class prior to December 7, 1941.

The story of how he became a naval aviation pilot is remarkable (no spoilers here). He flew over two hundred missions in VP-11, one of the first Black Cat Squadrons in the Pacific Theater. The planes were PBY-5 Catalinas and painted all black, with no markings at all. The squadron received a presidential unit citation:

> For outstanding performance above the normal call of duty while engaged in search missions and anti-shipping attacks in the enemy Japanese controlled area . . . locating enemy task force units and striking dangerously by night in devastating masthead, glide-bombing attacks to ensure vital hits on the target. Dauntless and aggressive in the fulfillment of each assignment, the gallant pilots of Squadron Eleven conducted daring, lone patrols regardless of weather . . . intercepting and attacking so effectively as to inflict substantial damage on hostile combat and other shipping, to deny the enemy the sea route . . .

Lou received his battlefield commission in the fall of 1943 in New Guinea. He was awarded the Distinguished Flying Cross for his role in the daring, multiday rescue mission, evacuating 219 Australian Coastwatchers and their equipment from the

Sepik River area of New Guinea as the enemy closed in on their position. He was shot down twice: once by the Japanese, once by friendly fire while on a mission to rescue the crew of a downed B-25 bomber. Remember the all-black aircraft?

He returned to the States and trained in the F7F Tigercat, a new twin-engine carrier-borne night fighter, for a return to combat. A personnel officer who knew Lou and his combat history saw his name on a list and said, "You've done enough," and he was placed in command of the Navy's first Target Drone Unit #1.

In the Korean War, he served on the aircraft carrier USS *Bon Homme Richard*, flying AD Sky Raiders on twenty-nine combat missions. He became the air intelligence officer for the carrier group and continued to grow his expertise in survival, escape, and evasion. His schooling was impressive. Lou felt that soldiers were more afraid of the jungle than the enemy and jumped at the chance to design and build the Navy's survival, escape and evasion, resistance to interrogation, espionage program (SERE). In conjunction with that assignment, he became the first naval officer to attend the new US Army's Special Operations School in Fort Bragg, North Carolina, in the fall of 1953. He was a classmate of several legendary Army officers. They would become lifelong friends and work together on what Lou refers to as "special jobs."

Lou personally established SERE classrooms around the world. He trained pilots on what to expect if they were shot down and captured. His training was usually ten to fourteen days long and tough. It prepared pilots for the treatment they would endure in North Vietnamese prison camps. It was his passion up to his retirement in 1967.

After retirement, he became a successful real estate broker and developer. After landing in Los Angeles, California, he rubbed elbows with notable business leaders and Hollywood celebrities, including Bob Hope, Bing Crosby, Jack Warner, and

Shirley Temple, to name a few. An avid and talented golfer, he played in six Bob Hope Desert Classics, winning the Pro-Am one year with Johnny Mathis in his foursome.

On April 26, 2017, Retired Lieutenant Commander Lou Conter was inducted into the Hall of Honor of the Maritime Patrol and Reconnaissance Forces located at Naval Air Station, Jacksonville, Florida. He recalled it was "the biggest honor of my ninety-five years of life." And, yes, at ninety-five, he personally attended the ceremony to receive the honor.

His lovely wife, Valerie, passed away on January 7, 2016. I continued to spend time with Lou when I realized that he had quietly filled a void in my life. He was four years older than my father would have been if he had survived past the age of sixty-five. Subconsciously, I had the same affection for and sense of comfort from Lou that people have for their own parents.

I was disappointed that the story of Lou Conter had not been formally recorded. Other soldiers and citizens had told their stories. I told him so. But in his mind, he had done nothing more than his duty. He had done his job. Also, he had participated in significant covert operations, which he had given his word not to talk about. His word is sacred, and he will never disclose the secret parts of his work. He does not like to see the books that are rolled out by former special operation servicemen within months of their retirement, talking about their exploits. Lou explains that those people gave their word, just as he did, that assignments, tactics, and other information were to be kept secret. Lou is a man of uncompromising integrity and has a continued sense of duty and responsibility.

In World War II, over sixteen million men and women served in the US military; each one has a story. Their service to the country ran between tedium and terror, stateside to the far parts of the globe. Many of those voices are now silent. We continue to lose our WWII veterans at an alarming rate. The Lou

Conter story is one such story, and it is an exceptional exploration of one man's journey through life. You may not be able to sit around his kitchen table and listen to him speak, but through this book, you can experience this man's life. I am so grateful to Lou Conter for allowing his story to be shared with a broader audience. It is an honor for me to use these pages to introduce this great American hero to you.

1

EARLY LIFE

I WAS BORN ON September 13, 1921, to Nicholas Anthony and Lottie Esther Conter. For the first year and a half of my life, I lived in a cabin that was built by my father and my Uncle Oscar on a forty-acre piece of property in Ojibwa, Wisconsin, located in the northern part of the state in Sawyer County on the banks of the Chippewa River.

I did not live for long in Ojibwa. We left in December of 1922 for New Mexico, where my father and uncle had been offered jobs as foremen on the crew that was working on the construction of Route 66, which became one of the most famous roads in the United States.

Route 66 originally ran from Chicago, Illinois, through Missouri, Kansas, Oklahoma, Texas, New Mexico, and Arizona before ending in Santa Monica in Los Angeles County, California, covering a total of 2,448 miles.

We made the trip from Wisconsin to New Mexico in a 1916 Lexington touring car. The car was packed, not just with my father; mother; older sister, Mary; and me but with every possession we owned. It took us a while to get where we were going. Not only were we traveling during the middle of winter, but Mother, who was pregnant at the time, ended up giving birth to my younger sister, Esther, on February 4, 1923, in Goodland, Kansas.

We ended up renting a train boxcar, which had been turned into a living unit, and we stayed in Goodland for ten days before traveling to Colorado Springs, Colorado.

From Colorado Springs, we made our way to Wolf Creek Pass in Colorado. For anyone not familiar with Wolf Creek Pass, it is a stretch of road that winds through the San Juan Mountains between South Fork, Colorado, and Pagosa Springs, Colorado. It was all dirt and gravel roads back then—very tricky and extremely dangerous. It took us three days to make it through Wolf Creek Pass. My uncle, whose family was traveling with us, ended up shooting a young deer so we could have some meat to eat during the trip. Somehow, we made it through the pass and into Durango, where we stayed with a cousin for a few days. Then we traveled on through Gallop, New Mexico, before reaching our final destination—Thoreau, New Mexico, which is about fifty miles east of Gallup on a Navajo Nation reservation.

After arriving in Thoreau, our first task was to get our living arrangements in order, which equated to putting up our tent and unpacking the car. I remember our beds were a blanket thrown on top of two feet of straw. The tent was not large, but our living space was comfortable.

The winters were a little rough but nothing that a wood-burning stove could not help to make a little better. The summers were tougher than the winters in many ways as there was not any air-conditioning back then, so the elements really came into play. The seasons were difficult, but when I think back on it, we really did not know any better; it was just the way life was.

My father and uncle oversaw the construction project, which included all the blasting and movement of rock and the paving of the highway. The dynamite tent was only about three hundred feet from our family tent, but we never felt as if we were in danger.

Mother and Aunt Ethel ran the mess tent. They did all the cooking for the road gang, which consisted of about forty men. They cooked on a woodstove and served breakfast, lunch, and dinner. The operation ran seven days a week and fifty-two weeks a year.

We lived in that tent in Thoreau for two years, and then, when it was time for Mary to start school, my parents decided to move. So, one day, we packed up our gear, got into the Lexington, and took off for Denver.

Once we got to Denver, my dad got a job at Swift & Company, which was a meatpacking company. He worked on the killing floor. If you have never been inside the workings of a meat-processing plant, it is not a pretty sight. The process is best described in *Wide-Open Town: Kansas City in the Pendergast Era* by Mutti Burke, Roe, and Herron:

> The process began with livestock driven into the factory where a "knocker" hit the animals with a heavy sledge, rendering them unconscious. Another worker attached the animal's hind legs to a mechanical hoist and then onto overhead rails. A "sticker" moved in and, in one quick motion, sliced the throat, causing the animal to bleed out. A team of knifemen, with sharp tools in each hand, then removed the animal's valuable hide.
>
> A "header" followed and detached the skull, a "gut-snatcher" took the intestines, and a "kidney puller" removed the animal's other internal organs. "Splitters," armed with heavy cleavers, sliced down the backbone, cutting the animals in two and, as the carcass moved across the killing floor, the animal was met by "rumpers,"

"backers," "grinders," "trimmers," "cheekers," "boners," "pullers," and "luggers," who processed the remaining meat.

A small Army of entry-level laborers helped the process along by moving carcasses, cutting off tails and horns, and cleaning up the blood.

Every job was a tough job, but Father was a hard worker, and he believed in giving his employers an honest day's work for an honest day's wage.

Father probably worked that job until 1927 or so; then we moved to Stockton, Kansas, to live with my uncle and his wife, who had settled on a small farm.

I attended school about five miles out of Stockton for my first three grades. The school was about a mile from our house, and it held thirteen kids in eight grades; we had one teacher and one classroom.

In 1930, we picked up again and moved back to Denver. Father got his job back at Swift & Company, and we also bought a twenty-acre farm about five miles outside of Denver. We had horses to pull the disks and the corn wagons, and we did all the plowing with hand plows. We grew sweet corn, cucumbers, and tomatoes.

During the summer, my job was to pull weeds from the fields, which I did, all day long. It was hard work, but it had to be done so that the crops could flourish. Twice a week, however, we would go to the market, where we sold our vegetables. Our bestselling crop was corn. We put eleven dozen ears of corn in a gunnysack and sold them for a dollar a sack. Having the farm allowed us to have food on our table and make a little extra money by selling some of our produce at the local markets.

During the school year, I would come home from school, and Mother would usually say, "Louis, you better go out and kill a couple of rabbits so we can have some meat for dinner with potatoes and white gravy." So, at seven years old, I would go out, shoot a couple of rabbits, dress them out, and bring them into the house, where Mother would cut them up and cook them for dinner.

We were about a year into the Depression (which began in August 1929), so what you have to remember is that the people who were fortunate enough to have a job were getting paid very minimally—only about thirty cents an hour. They would work eight hours a day, which meant they were taking home thirteen to fourteen dollars a week.

Times were tough, but we had access to food on a consistent basis, which was more than what many people had during those times. We felt extremely fortunate. Compared to many people, we had it good.

Father was fortunate; the folks at Swift & Company had taken a shine to him early in his life and remained loyal to him throughout the years. My father was a good employee, and because of his work ethic, the vice president of Swift & Company kept him working.

From 1931 to 1937, I walked to school, which was located just outside of Denver; it was five miles each way. I tried out for the football team, not necessarily because I loved football but because I could use the showers at the school after practice. At home, we did not have running water; we had to pull a tub out in the kitchen, close the doors, and heat the water on the woodstove to take a bath. That was not much fun, especially with two sisters.

During my junior year, we sold the farm and moved to Wheatridge, which was right next to Denver. My walk from our house to school was only a mile and a half, which made life much easier. There was a large mountain lion population in the area, so I always carried my rifle to school just in case I ever crossed paths with one. I saw a few mountain lions but never had to shoot one.

I spent my junior and senior years at Wheatridge. During the summers, I ended up helping my uncle work his farm, which was about 120 acres; again, it was hard work, but that was all I knew.

I decided to see if I could go to work at Swift & Company. At that time, a hundred men were waiting in line at a quarter to seven in the morning, just hoping a worker would not show. If someone did not show up for work, they were immediately replaced by one of the men waiting in the line. I got lucky, however, because the vice president of Swift & Company liked my dad and knew he was a hard worker, and he knew that I was a hard worker as well, so he hired me.

I was a senior in high school, and I was working as a cleaner on the killing floor. Every Friday night, we were given an envelope with our week's pay. The envelope contained one ten-dollar bill and two one-dollar bills.

After a short period of time, I became a hide shaker. After the knifemen removed the hide, the shaking of the cowhides took place in the cellar. Shaking cowhides is a job that is exactly what it sounds like. Four men each took a corner of the cowhide, and we would shake it by popping it up and down. It was a physically demanding job, and we did this for eight hours a day. Even though I was only seventeen at the time, I was able to keep up with the older guys. It was a hard job, but it was a good job.

In September of 1939, I turned eighteen. In October, our neighbor Dooley Wick came home on ninety days of leave. Dooley's brother, Tom was a friend of mine with whom I played football, and Dooley had joined the Navy four years before. He was a signalman third class on the USS *Nevada* when his enlistment was up in 1939.

Back then, if you reenlisted within that ninety-day leave

period, you would get your same rate back and go back to the fleet. His ninety days were just about up, so he asked Tom and me if we would go down to the recruiter so he could sign up for another four years.

I was working the swing shift, which was from 3:30 p.m. until 11:00 p.m., and as I mentioned earlier, like most men, I was earning thirty cents an hour. So when I found out that the Navy was paying seventeen dollars a month, I thought it probably could not hurt to listen to what they had to say.

We went down with him, and, naturally, the recruiter grabbed us and gave us the entrance exams and had us take physicals. Of course, we all passed the exams, but at that time, there was an eight-to-nine-month waiting list to get into apprentice seaman boot camp in San Diego, California, so I went back to work, did not say anything to anyone, and to be honest, I really did not think much about it.

About two weeks later, at 8:15 a.m., Mother came up to my room and said, "Are you in trouble, Louis?" I said, "No. Why?" She said, "Someone is on the phone from the government and wants to talk to Louis Anthony Conter."

So I went downstairs, picked up the phone, and said hello. The voice on the other end said, "Hello, this is the US Navy Department. We have a draft of men scheduled to go out tonight at five forty-five. We are short six men, and we need to fill their positions. Can you come down and talk to us?"

I was supposed to be at work at three-thirty that afternoon, so I went down early and stopped at the Navy Department. They said, "If you agree to enlist for four years, we will give you room and board and seventeen dollars a month."

I thought about it for a minute and then thought, *What the heck? It's only four years.* Then I could get out, go back to college, and be better off for the football team at the University of Colorado. So I signed up.

I called my girlfriend, Marfaye Ammons, and broke the news to her. While she was heartbroken about my leaving, she supported me. Marfaye's father was Teller Ammons, whose brother was the governor of Colorado at the time. Ammons had a successful but short term as governor. During his two-year tenure, the State Water Conservation Board and the State Game and Fish Department were founded. The State Industrial School was restructured, the Big Thompson Highway was opened, and employment opportunities increased through the Works Progress Administration.

Mother was supportive, but I could tell she would have rather I stayed at home. As the only son, I would like to think I was her favorite. My sisters would probably disagree.

I called Swift & Company and told them I had joined the Navy and was leaving that night at quarter to six. They told me to come down so they could pay me for the hours I had worked. I picked up my envelope. It had eight dollars in it.

When I arrived at the train station, my mother and father were waiting for me. We said our goodbyes, and at exactly 5:45 p.m., the train whistle blew. I stepped aboard the train.

As the train started to move, I suddenly realized that was it. I was leaving. I was taking my first train ride, and I was going from Denver, Colorado, to San Diego, California. I had joined the US Navy and was off to boot camp.

2

I'm in the Navy

On September 5, 1939, a few days after German forces marched into Poland, the president proclaimed the neutrality of the United States. So by the time I entered the Navy, the war had broken out in Europe, and I was fully aware that even though Franklin D. Roosevelt, who was president at the time, proclaimed US neutrality, most everyone knew it was only a matter of time before we would be forced to choose a side. It was also no surprise that we would not be on the side of the Germans.

Every person who enlisted, no matter what branch, went through basic training, or bootcamp, as most people call it. There were four Naval Training Stations before the start of WWII: Newport, Rhode Island; Great Lakes, Illinois; Norfolk, Virginia; and San Diego, California. On November 15, 1939, I reported to the Naval Training Station (NTS) in San Diego for basic training.

The San Diego NTS was established during World War I. In 1917, it took the form of a tent camp in the city's Balboa Park, but immediately after the war, a permanent training station was established north of the city on a tract of land overlooking the bay.

The new station was commissioned in 1923. The one I attended was not very big as it was comprised of four barracks, some trade-school buildings, and an auditorium, but by 1939, the station had facilities enough to provide accommodations for five thousand recruits.

After riding the train all night from Colorado, I arrived in San Diego the next day. The Navy had a petty officer waiting for us, and as soon we got off the train, he said, "Stand at attention." Well, most of us did not know what that meant, but we learned quickly.

When we arrived on base, we discarded our civilian attire and our possessions. After standing in a large room with hundreds of other young men in nothing but our skivvies, we began to make our way through a supply line, where a Navy supply clerk tossed us the uniforms and other gear we would use during our entire enlistment.

The clerks handed us our uniforms—with little attention to size—along with sleeping gear, mattress covers, a pillow, two pillow covers, and two blankets. We took all these items and stuffed them into a cylindrical canvas sack called a seabag that was three feet long by two feet wide. The seabag had grommets on top, through which we wove a line to use as a drawstring to close the bag and hang it from our racks.

Our seabag contained everything we had to our names. Speaking of names, we stenciled our names on everything—on the side of the bag, on our shirts, on our pants, even on our underwear. I would later learn that my seabag went with me everywhere. I could pack up my seabag, sling it over my shoulder, and march off with all my worldly possessions.

We had our heads shaved, were issued serial numbers, and were assigned to a group and to our barracks, where we would meet the other members of our platoon. We slept, ate, learned, and trained together.

We did hours of physical fitness training as a unit and practiced the same basic skills over and over and over and over again. We marched, loaded, unloaded, and cleaned our weapons. We polished our shoes, shined our brass, and made sure our gig lines were always lined up and ready for inspection. We did not have beds (or bunks); rather, we had hammocks.

Drill instructors used tough methods and forced us to pay attention to details and protocol. Even the smallest mistakes by a recruit could result in extra duty, usually in the kitchen, or it sometimes involved a challenging physical punishment. There were times when repeated offenses by the same recruit resulted in the entire unit being disciplined.

The primary goal of boot camp was to teach recruits to think of themselves not as an individual but more as a member of a unit. Basic training was all about training people to work seamlessly with one another to achieve the objective of the unit.

There have been many tales told of the horrors of Navy boot camp, but to be honest, boot camp was not extremely hard for me. I was in excellent shape, I liked to work hard, and I could follow instructions; I thought it was a pretty simple process. I understood what the Navy was asking me to do—they wanted me to be prepared to do what they asked when they asked.

I did not mind boot camp as much as some of the others; I looked at the entire experience with a positive attitude. Sure, we lost all our hair, but we did not have to pay the barber; yes, it is true that we were given so many shots that most of us felt like pin cushions, but that just meant that there was not a disease out there that would affect me. Best of all, however, we were given three meals a day, and I did not have to go hunting to make sure we ate. Boot camp was not hard.

The first few weeks were simple. We marched, we marched

some more, and then, when we were done marching, we marched again. We marched everywhere we went.

Marching was easy; if you could listen to commands, you could march. Forward march, mark time, march, half step, march, column right (or column left), march, to the rear; march, change step, march, right (or left) step, march, right flank (or left flank), march. If you knew what these commands meant, and you were in decent physical shape, you breezed through this part of boot camp. I was used to walking many miles, so the marching was just a matter of paying attention to what commands were being given.

After ten days or so, the Marine master sergeant said to me, "Conter, you are not getting tired. Why is that?" I answered back, "This is easy walking, and where I come from, we are used to walking. I used to walk in the mountains and hunt mountain lions." He pulled me out of the ranks and made me a squadron leader.

The guys from the city struggled a little with the walking. You must keep in mind that we were walking six, seven, eight hours a day. If you were not used to that type of exercise, it was challenging to keep up with those of us who were.

During those first few weeks, we received all our shots, complete dental and medical exams, and had some basic schooling. We were taught the right way to fold and store our new belongings and how to stow our hammocks.

The next three weeks were filled with more physical conditioning, swimming, drilling, and, most importantly, attending Navy classes, where we learned not only the Navy way but a thing or two about naval history. We also had mess duty, which was washing dishes in the scullery, food prep, mess deck cleaning, and/or line server duty.

We also engaged in activities at the gunnery range. I was good with a rifle, so the training was fun for me. We learned the basics of range safety: 1) treat every weapon as if it were loaded; 2) keep your finger straight and off the trigger until you intend to fire; 3) never point your weapon at anything you do not intend to shoot; 4) keep your weapon on safe until you intend to fire. Pretty simple rules, easy to follow, especially for someone who had been around a rifle from an early age.

Boot camp was all about learning to be a part of a team, where every man's life depended on how well the man next to him learned to do his job. Boot camp also taught us three important words—words that were, and still are, at the very core of Navy values. The words that became ideals that many, if not all, of us came to live by were honor, courage, and commitment. The words mean different things to different people.

I believe honor means we do everything the best we can. I believe courage means that no matter the danger or the fear, one should enter into every job no matter what. Do not ever panic, never, or you are dead. Remember where you are. I believe commitment means get the job done no matter what.

These three principles have served me well throughout my life, and I strongly believe they can serve our future generations just as well. Ask any Sailor or Marine what these words mean to them, and I am confident their answers will impress you.

In January of 1940, I completed boot camp and was given orders to report aboard the USS *Arizona* for duty. There were five or six from my boot camp squadron that were assigned to the USS *Arizona*. We packed our hammocks and seabags and were taken to Long Beach pier, where a liberty boat from the USS *Arizona* picked us up and took us to the ship. With our hammocks and seabags over our shoulders, we went up the gangplank, faced aft to salute, and told the officer of the deck we had orders to report aboard for duty.

I was assigned to Division 2 and was sent to stow my gear. Then I reported to the deck of the USS *Arizona* (BB-39) for duty.

3

MY FIRST SHIP,
THE USS *ARIZONA*

THE USS *ARIZONA* WAS a magnificent ship. She was what is
known as a Pennsylvania-class ship—a super-dreadnought battleship built just before the First World War. There were only
two Pennsylvania-class ships, the USS *Arizona*, and the USS
Pennsylvania, which were named after their respective states. The
USS *Arizona* was a large ship. Its overall length was 608 feet,
which is the equivalent of two football fields. The beam (width)
of the ship was ninety-seven feet. The keel was laid on March
16, 1913, and was launched on June 19, 1915.

They say over seventy-five thousand people attended the
launch, including John Purroy Mitchel, the mayor of New York
City; George W. P. Hunt, the governor of Arizona; and several other high-ranking officials and dignitaries. Esther Ross, who
was the seventeen-year-old daughter of William Ross, a prominent businessman in Prescott, Arizona, was selected by Governor Hunt to do the honors of christening the ship.

In 1914, the Arizona state legislature and voters had passed
a bill to ban alcohol sales and consumption, thereby enacting a
prohibition that went into effect on January 1, 1915, five years

before the national ban on alcohol began (Arizona Republic, 2014). To appease the Arizona politicians and the Arizona temperance movement, the Navy agreed to use two bottles to christen the USS *Arizona*, one filled with champagne, which was the tradition, and a second bottle filled with water drawn from the Roosevelt Dam, which is on the Salt River located northeast of Phoenix.

There were rumblings from some circles that breaking from ancient seafaring traditions would bring bad luck to the USS *Arizona*; regardless, Esther Ross swung both bottles toward the ship as it slid from its holding blocks and proclaimed, "I christen thee *Arizona*!"

By the time I had seen the USS *Arizona* for the first time, she already had a long career and had gone through a few modernizations. I think what made the battleships of that time so impressive were their big guns; the USS *Arizona* had twelve forty-five caliber, fourteen-inch guns housed in triple-gun turrets. Each gun rested within an armored turret, which protruded above the main deck. Each turret extended four decks below, except for turret two, which extended five decks down. The turrets were numbered one through four, running from bow to stern. The lower spaces held the equipment that was needed to elevate the guns and rotate the turret. At the bottom of each turret was the handling room that contained the powder bags and projectiles.

The USS *Arizona* carried one hundred shells (projectiles) for each gun; fourteen hundred shells were always carried aboard the ship. Each shell weighed about fourteen hundred pounds. The ship also had twelve fifty-one-caliber, five-inch guns mounted in individually fortified gun emplacement structures built into the sides of the hull. She additionally had eight twenty-five-caliber, five-inch guns for counter-air defense and two twenty-one-inch torpedo tubes with a ship's allotment of twenty-four torpedoes.

When I reported aboard the USS *Arizona*, I did so as an

apprentice seaman. I was in the Second Division and was a deck force seaman. I was assigned to turret number two as my general quarters' station, and like every new sailor, I served my time in the galley as a mess cook.

Captain Isaac C. Kidd was our skipper. Captain Kidd, who was soon to be Admiral Kidd, was a graduate of the US Naval Academy and had been aboard battleships for a great part of his career. Kidd participated in the 1907–1909 Great White Fleet cruise around the world while serving on the battleship USS *New Jersey*. He became the aide and flag secretary to the commander in chief of the Pacific Fleet, the first of his many flagstaff assignments. He served a few tours of duty as an instructor at the US Naval Academy and as a staff member at the Naval War College, which he had attended in the mid-1930s (Gibson, 2020).

Kidd was the commanding officer of the USS *Arizona* from September 1938 until February 1940, when he was promoted to rear admiral and assigned as commander battleship Division One and chief of staff to commander, Battleships, Battle Force (Gibson, 2020).

I only had Captain Kidd as a skipper for a few weeks before Captain Harold C. Train assumed command of the ship on February 3, 1940. Captain Train, like Captain Kidd, graduated from the US Naval Academy. During World War I, Train was assigned to the Office of Naval Communications, Navy Department in Washington, DC. He went overseas in March 1918, when he was assigned as executive officer of the USS *Siboney*, which was tasked with transporting troops to Europe.

During my first few months aboard the USS *Arizona*, life was very routine. We got up at 5:30 a.m., had breakfast, and reported on deck for the hoisting of the flag, which took place at 8:00 a.m. From there, we reported to our different stations, which, aboard a battleship, consisted of scrubbing decks, shining brass, and whatever the senior petty officer told us to do. We also drilled our battle stations.

As I mentioned earlier, my general quarters' station was the lower powder handling room of turret two, which later blew up in the attack on Pearl Harbor on December 7, 1941. The powder handling room is at the very bottom of the turret. In that room, three powder door operators and nine powder bag passers worked together to place the powder bags onto a powder hoist.

The powder hoist then moved the powder bags to the scuttle operators, who took the 105-pound powder bag from the magazine scuttle and then handed them to the powder passers. The powder passer would place the powder bag into the powder car, and when the car contained six bags, the doors closed, and the car moved up through the hoist trunk to the gun room. I was a powder passer, and while the work in the powder handling room was hard, it was not any harder than being a hide shaker.

In March of 1940, we departed from Long Beach, California, and made our way to Hawaii. By April of 1940, we had joined up with the Pacific Fleet and engaged in maneuvers around Hawaii.

When I was at my general quarters' station, and well below deck, the guns sounded like a very faint rumble, but if anyone was on the decks closer to the top deck of the ship, look out. The sound of the fourteen-inch guns going off in a crescendo of explosions is breathtaking, and the sound is ferocious. The eruption of yellow flame and black smoke that blew out of each gun barrel's end was equally impressive.

When we returned to Honolulu, the crew was told that we would not be going back to the west coast but would remain in Pearl Harbor. From the time the Pacific Fleet was established until May 1940, the primary bases for the US Fleet had been stationed at Long Beach and San Diego, with Pearl Harbor serving as an advance base and a concentration point during maneuvers, but that changed when the Empire of Japan was growing more militaristic and expansionist. President Roosevelt and his advisers decided that moving the fleet to Hawaii was a show of power and deterrent to Japan; they also believed should hostilities break out, the United States would be in a far better position to respond.

During my off hours, I would study manuals. I was studying for seaman first class. In June 1940, our chief quartermaster, Robert Sink, noticed I was not going ashore much and that I liked to study and read. He asked me if I would like to be a quartermaster striker. I knew some of the duties of a quartermaster, and I also knew they did not scrub decks. I jumped at the opportunity.

A week later, I was transferred from the Second Division to the navigation division (N division), and I became a quartermaster striker. Most people think of a quartermaster as someone responsible for providing quarters, rations, clothing, and other supplies, which, in other branches of the service and the civilian world, is correct. In the Navy, however, a quartermaster is an enlisted member who oversees the watch-to-watch navigation of the ship. While the ship is underway, quartermasters keep logs down to the minute. They stand watch on the bridge alongside the officer of the deck. They are also responsible for navigational instruments and clocks and training the ship's lookouts and helmsmen.

In port, the quartermaster reports to the quarterdeck between turret three and the mainmast, where the gangplanks are set to accept personnel who are either departing from or arriving at the ship. Quartermasters perform these duties under the control of the ship's navigator or the officer of the deck if there is no navigation officer.

I had to learn the maintenance, correction, and preparation of nautical charts and navigation publications. I also had to learn to work with charts and grids and all about longitude and latitude—but you know something? The job was a thousand times better than working on the killing floor at Swift & Company.

In July 1940, we joined several other ships in the Pacific Fleet and visited several islands in the South Sea. Our trip to Christmas Island, Palmyra Island, and Jarvis Island was intended to be a show of force to the Japanese, who were involved in the Second World War and invaded China.

It was on this trip that I crossed the equator for the first time, which meant that I went from being a pollywog to a shellback. I do not think anyone knows when or how the line crossing ceremony came about, but the ritual has been around for many, many years; the equator crossing ritual is known as the Order of Neptune and is one of the most storied stories in Western seafaring. The ceremony observes a mariner's transformation from pollywog, a seaman who has not crossed the equator, to a dependable, trustworthy, and reliable shellback, or a son of Neptune (Pelley, 2020).

When a ship crosses the equator, King Neptune comes aboard to exercise authority over his domain and to judge charges brought against pollywogs that they are only posing as sailors and have not paid proper homage to the god of the sea. High-ranking members of the crew and those who have been shellbacks the longest dress up in elaborate costumes, and each is a member of King Neptune's court. For instance, the ship's captain might play the part of King Neptune himself. What proceeds is a day of festivities that builds camaraderie among the seafaring crew (Moore, 2013).

As pollywogs, we were required to put on a talent show with dancing, songs, skits, or poetry. We had to eat amazingly spicy food and were forced to stand before a court of seasoned shellbacks to answer a variety of charges and appear before King Neptune. We were asked to wear our clothes inside out or backward and crawl across the deck through nasty, disgusting, and odious debris. In some cases, a wog would be ordered to crawl on his hands and knees to the royal baby, who was one of the hairiest, most obese shellbacks on the ship, kiss his lard-covered stomach, and eat a maraschino cherry out of his navel (Salty Old Dog School, 2020).

All in all, the line crossing ceremony/Order of Neptune was good fun. Heck, even Franklin D. Roosevelt, the president of the United States, went through the line crossing ceremony in 1936 when he was aboard the USS *Indianapolis*. According to Chen (2020):

> In late November of 1936, when the USS *Indianapolis* crossed the Equator with President Franklin Roosevelt aboard, even the leader of a nation was not subject to an exemption. Roosevelt was made to plead his case before a seasoned sailor who dressed up as King Neptune and had to go through some degree of embarrassment before he was granted the status of a Shellback. Like most sailors who went through this rite of passage, Roosevelt was given a certificate to show his status as a trusty Shellback.

For the most part, the line crossing ceremony was a lot of fun, more so if you were a shellback. Once the ceremony is complete, pollywogs receive a certificate declaring their new status. Being a shellback and having that certificate meant a lot to many of us; it's a shame that some of us lost our certificates on December 7, 1941.

In September 1940, we returned to Long Beach and made our way up the coast to the Puget Sound Navy Yard in Bremerton, Washington, for a three-month overhaul. While the ship was being overhauled, the crew did all the maintenance of the ship. We scraped the hull, painted, overhauled the engines, and took care of all the general housekeeping duties needed to keep a ship like the USS *Arizona* battle-ready.

During this refit, the foundation for a search radar was added atop her foremast, her antiaircraft directors were upgraded, and a platform for four water-cooled .50-inch (12.7mm) caliber M2 Browning machine guns was installed at the very top of the mainmast.

I took ten days of leave in November 1940 to attend my younger sister Esther's wedding. It was good to get home for a while, and it was nice to see my folks and a few friends.

I even met up with Marfaye, who was my girlfriend before I joined the Navy. When we were going out, I gave Marfaye a ring. Since I left on such short notice when I joined the Navy, I did not think about asking her for it back before I left. She gave it back to me during my visit with her. It was nice of her to return the ring; I was not expecting her to do so. I took it back to the jeweler and exchanged it for a nice watch.

I returned to the USS *Arizona* in early December. In January of 1941, I made seaman first class. My pay jumped from thirty-six to fifty-four dollars a month. I couldn't believe I was making that much money. On January 23, 1941, Rear Admiral Isaac C. Kidd returned to the USS *Arizona* when he was named commander, Battleship Division One, and he designated the USS *Arizona* as his flagship. We departed Bremerton, Washington, in late January, and I was assigned as the quartermaster of the watch. I kept the log with the duty officer, and while on watch, we logged comings and goings of anyone boarding or leaving the ship. When we left the channel, I was the channel helmsman and steered/navigated the ship in and out of port.

We arrived in Pearl Harbor on February 3, 1941. A few days later, Captain Train left the USS *Arizona* to become chief of staff with Battle Force.

During the Japanese attack on Pearl Harbor, Train issued

orders for the battleship USS *Nevada* not to sortie so as to minimize the damage to the ship and avert the possibility of its sinking and blocking the Pearl Harbor channel. For his conduct during the attack, Train was awarded the Navy Commendation Medal with Combat "V" from the commander of the Pacific Fleet, Admiral Chester W. Nimitz. Train ultimately rose to the rank of rear admiral and was assigned to the Joint Post-War Committee within the Joint Chiefs of Staff in Washington, DC. He retired from the Navy on May 1, 1946, and lived to the age of eighty (Wikipedia, 2020).

As we started the new year, the war in Europe was raging. There was a split in opinion between many Americans as to whether the United States should join the war or not. Many Americans wanted to remain neutral and avoid getting pulled into another "European" problem. Americans were divided over what the role of the United States in the war should be or if it should even have a role at all. To be honest with you, those of us in the military knew the United States would be headed to war; we just did not know when.

4

ALOHA, HAWAII

ON FEBRUARY 5, 1941, two days after we had arrived in Pearl Harbor, Hawaii, Franklin Van Valkenburgh became the commanding officer of the USS *Arizona* (BB-39). As were most of our commanding officers, Van Valkenburgh was a graduate of the US Naval Academy, class of 1909. After serving on the battleship USS *Vermont* (BB-20) and on the USS *South Carolina,* Van Valkenburgh was commissioned ensign on June 5, 1911. Traveling to the Asiatic station soon after that, he joined the submarine tender USS *Rainbow* (AS-7) at Olongapo, Philippine Islands, on September 11. He reported to the gunboat USS *Pampanga* (PG-39) as executive officer on June 23, 1914, for a short tour in the southern Philippines before his detachment on August 4, 1914.

After returning to the United States, Lt. (JG.) Van Valkenburgh joined the USS *Connecticut* (BB-18) on November 11, 1914. Following postgraduate work in steam engineering at the Naval Academy in September 1915, he took further instruction in that field at Columbia University before reporting to the USS *Rhode Island* (BB-17) on March 2, 1917. The entry of the United States into World War I found Van Valkenburgh serving as the battleship's engineering officer. Subsequent temporary duty on the receiving ship at New York preceded his first tour as an instructor at the Naval Academy. On June 1, 1920, Van Valkenburgh reported onboard USS *Minnesota* (BB-22) for duty as an engineer officer, and he held that post until the battleship was decommissioned in November 1921 (USNA Virtual Memorial Hall, 2020).

He again served as an instructor at the Naval Academy until May 15, 1925, before joining USS *Maryland* (BB-46) on June 26, 1925. He was commissioned as commander on June 2, 1927, while in Maryland. He soon reported for duty in the Office of the Chief of Naval Operations on May 21, 1928, and served there during the administrations of Admirals Charles F. Hughes and William V. Pratt. Van Valkenburgh detached on June 28, 1931, received command of the destroyer USS *Talbot* (DD-114) on July 10, 1931, and commanded Destroyer Squadron 5 from March 31, 1932 (USNA Virtual Memorial Hall, 2020).

After he attended the Naval War College in Newport, Rhode Island, and completed the senior course in May 1934, Comdr. Van Valkenburgh served as inspector of naval material at the New York Navy Yard before going to sea again as commanding officer of USS *Melville* (AD-2) from June 8, 1936, to June 11, 1938. He was promoted to captain while commanding *Melville* on December 23, 1937. He served as the inspector of material for the Third Naval District from August 6, 1938, to January 22, 1941, before taking command of the USS *Arizona* (USNA Virtual Memorial Hall, 2020).

Changes in leadership at the ship level were not the only changes that were made. In February of 1941, Admiral Husband E. Kimmel was named commander in chief, United States Fleet (CINCUS). Kimmel was also appointed commander in chief, US Pacific Fleet (CINCPACFLT). Much has been said about Admiral Kimmel and his role regarding the attack on Pearl Harbor.

Was he a good leader? Was he a bad leader? All I can tell you is that we drilled and prepared constantly. The training and the efficiency of the USS *Arizona*, and the fleet as a whole, was very high. Even William "Bull" Halsey, who, in 1941, commanded one of the Pacific Fleet's carrier task forces and rose during the war to five-star fleet admiral, described Kimmel as "the ideal man for the job" (Halsey, 1947). The bottom line was the higher-ups, including Admiral Kimmel, knew war was coming. They just did not know when or where.

So from February 1941 through much of the spring and early summer, life fell into a routine. We were constantly in and out of port. We were involved in maneuvers almost weekly and then were back in port for a few days. When we were in port, I tried to spend as much time as I could with my girlfriend, Helen "Hester" Hitchcock.

I had met Hester at a dance in the spring of 1940 when she was a junior at Punahou School. By the end of the night, she had given me her phone number. About a week after the dance, I gave her a call. She invited me to dinner so I could meet her family, or, more accurately, so that I could meet her father. Hester's father was Harvey Hitchcock, and he was a very influential man in Hawaii. Mr. Hitchcock, who was born in Honolulu, was a fourth-generation descendant of two prominent missionary families: the Judds (Gerrit Parmele) on his mother's side and the Hitchcocks (Harvey Rexford) on his father's side.

Mr. Hitchcock was the son of David Howard Hitchcock, a painter known for his depictions of Hawaii. A few years back, I read that one of David Hitchcock's paintings, titled *Windward Oahu, Hawaii* (a twelve—by-eighteen-inch oil painting on canvas), sold for $82,250.

Hester's father graduated from Punahou School and Cornell University and was employed by the Hawaiian Dredging Company and Dillingham Corporation from 1922 until his retirement in 1964. He was an executive in the company and may even have been a part-owner; I'm not sure. But his family had been in Hawaii for a long time, so he was a well-respected man.

The dinner went well. Mr. Hitchcock must have approved of me because shortly after that dinner, Hester's parents gave me my own room at the house so I could keep a change of clothing and not worry about going back to ship during my weekend liberties.

Hester was a great gal. She had a great personality and was fun to be around. We did what young people living in Hawaii did in the 1940s; we went to dances, spent time on Waikiki Beach, and hung out at her house.

I was so fortunate to have Hester's family in my life during my time in Hawaii. They treated me like a son, and for that, I have been grateful for my entire life. I tried to spend as much time as possible with Hester and her family, just for a sense of normalcy. It was nice to be in a family environment.

With whatever other free time I had, I cracked the books. The quartermaster third class exam was coming up, and I wanted to make sure I did everything I could to pass it. In early June of 1941, I sat for my quartermaster third class exam and was extremely excited to have passed.

On June 11, 1941, we departed from Pearl Harbor for Long Beach, California. We arrived a few days later. It was not a long trip, and we would make our return trip to Hawaii a few weeks later.

While we were in Long Beach, we were joined by a new group of sailors, including twenty-one musicians who were members of Unit Band 22. The band members were recent graduates of the Navy School of Music and had been assigned duty aboard the USS *Arizona*.

On their very first day aboard ship, they performed, and from the get-go, I knew they were something special. They brought a sense of home to all of us.

While, yes, they were musicians, they were also sailors, and they had been assigned to a battle station just like the rest of us. The band had a special place in my heart as it was assigned to the powder handling room in turret number two, which was my first battle station when I arrived aboard the USS *Arizona*.

The band members never played when we were at sea; instead, they manned their duty stations. It was another story when we were in port as they played constantly. If they were not playing a concert on the ship or in the community, they were practicing aboard. Since my duty station was on deck, and the band always performed near the fantail, I watched them all the time. I liked them, and, as we learned, they were one of the best bands in the fleet.

On July 1, 1941, we departed Long Beach, and we arrived in Pearl Harbor on July 8, 1941. Once we were back in Pearl Harbor, it was a return to the grind for most of July and August as we continued with our routine training exercises. We conducted short-range target practice, torpedo defense practice, battle practice, and even prepared for an air attack at sea.

The USS *Arizona* was supposed to return to San Pedro, California, in September for another overhaul, but a British ship that had been pretty beaten up in battle against the Germans ended up taking our place. It was a disappointment for most of the crew not to be heading to California. Rumor had it that the USS *Arizona* was slated for a refit in December, so we would be returning stateside soon.

Fleet recreation did a fantastic job serving the military. There were baseball, softball, and football fields throughout and around the bases. There were dozens of tennis courts, handball courts, volleyball courts, basketball courts, and swimming pools that could be used by the military personnel and their families. There was even a golf course, which was reserved for officers. Fleet recreation also arranged a variety of competitions, including musical, athletic, and even rodeo competitions.

In September 1941, I was a member of the USS *Arizona* football team. The USS *Arizona* had a rich football tradition. The big year for football was 1935. All-American Buzz Borries put the finishing touch on a team that was talented already. Enlisted men such as Carl Gleason, Charles Rourk, and John Hostinksky had been on the squad since the ship went back into service in 1931. The coach was Lt. Hank Hardwick, who later coached the Naval Academy (The Greater Northwest Football Association, 2020).

Our schedule was not too involved in 1941; we played teams from other ships, battleships for the most part. We had an eight-to-ten-game schedule. I played halfback, and while I was not a Byron "Whizzer" White or a George McAfee of National Football League fame, I was not half bad, and I had a lot of fun playing.

The Richardson Recreation Center, located on the eastern shore of Pearl Harbor, was built to serve Navy personnel on visiting ships as well as those based on the installation. During the war years, ships ran hourly liberty boats to this center, which was open from 0900 to 1800 daily. The center offered the largest freshwater swimming pool on the island and playing fields and facilities for baseball, softball, track, tennis, handball, archery, boxing, and wrestling. Intramural teams from the ships played baseball or softball in the morning, barbecued food brought from the ships and picnicked in areas adjacent to the playing fields, and then swam in the pool. The clubhouse also had a canteen and dance floor, and dances were held every two weeks. The recreational facilities were significant for their role in building morale among Pearl Harbor personnel during WWII (National Park Service—Department of the Interior, 2004).

The Bloch Recreation Center and Arena, which was named after Rear Admiral Claude C. Bloch, who was commandant of the Pearl Harbor Naval Base and the Fourteenth Naval District, was another facility that supplemented the Richardson Recreation Center. Bloch Recreation Center and Arena was intended for use both by personnel throughout the base and by those on visiting ships. It was centrally located near the main gate and could accommodate six thousand spectators for concerts, stage performances, boxing matches, and movies. It featured a large basketball court undercover, ten bowling alleys, six pool tables, reading and writing rooms, a canteen and beer bar, and a dance floor.

In September 1941, Fleet services organized a competition for the bands called the Battle of Music, featuring seventeen Navy bands and one US Marine Corps barracks band. The Battle of Music was held every two weeks and featured Navy bands from capitol ships homeported in Pearl Harbor and bands attached to shore installations in Hawaii. Four bands compete in each round for the chance to compete in the final round of the competition. Each band competed with a swing number, a ballad, and a specialty tune and performed for a jitterbug contest.

On September 13, 1941, the first round of the competition was held with the USS *Arizona* band and bands from the USS *West Virginia* and the USS *California*. The band from the submarine base competed with the USS *Arizona* band and took top honors.

Fleet recreation knew their role was to help provide military personnel and their families with a taste of home, and there was no better way of doing that than to have these types of athletic and musical programs available. They wanted us to have a chance to have fun, blow off some steam, and have some normalcy in our lives.

It was also in mid-September that a friend of mine from Texas, B. J. Johnston, and I started talking about getting into flight school. B. J. was a fifth division gunner's mate and one of my football teammates, and one day he said, "Lou, let's sign up for flight school. I said, "Flight school? I've never been in a plane. And we're right-arm rates, so they will never take us." A right-arm rate meant we strictly did seagoing jobs.

A few weeks later, I was at Hester's house for dinner, and in walked Admiral W. L. Calhoun, the base force commander for Pearl Harbor, who just happened to be one of Hester's father's good friends.

Like all admirals, Admiral Calhoun had an impressive ré-sumé. A graduate of the Naval Academy, Calhoun had a tre-mendous career on land and sea. In January 1938, he became chief of staff and aide to commander Battleships, Battle Force. In November 1938, he was commissioned rear admiral and at-tended the advanced course at the Naval War College at for six months, and in December 1939, became Commander Base Force, US Fleet, re-designated as Base Force, Pacific Fleet, in February 1941.

The admiral asked me what my rate was, and I said, "I'm a third-class quartermaster on the USS *Arizona*, sir." The fact that I was on a battleship gave him a reason to smile.

Eventually, the conversation turned to my future plans, so I took the opportunity to share with the admiral that I was inter-ested in flight school; however, because I was a right-arm rate, I doubted I would be eligible for admission.

The admiral smiled and said, "Conter, there is no law against any rating going to flight school as long as you pass the exams. The requests come in through me, and I'm the one who signs the orders. Take the exam; see if you pass." I had a new goal, and the next day, I began studying for my exams to get into flight school.

I took my exam in September and was told the results should be back by late October or early November. I thought I had done well, but only time would tell.

We went back out to sea in mid-September, and during this trip, I took my first airplane ride. World War II battleships often carried a scout or surveillance plane. The USS *Arizona* carried a Vought OS2U Kingfisher, which was a single-engine mono-plane (mid-wing). The plane had a large central float and two small stabilizing floats. It was a catapult-launched plane known as "the eyes of the fleet" due to the crew of the aircraft directing the gunfire coming from the ship. The Vought OS2U Kingfisher was not only used for surveillance but also played a significant role in air-sea rescue operations due to its ability to land and take off from the water. It did not have much power, but it was a durable plane and a perfect fit for a battleship.

Before my inaugural flight, Lieutenant Ragsdale, the senior pilot on the ship, gave me instructions on what to do as a back-seat passenger. Then, after I was provided with a quick overview of base-safety protocols and how to use a parachute, I took my place in the plane and was shot off the number three catapult.

It was a clear day, and there was not much wind for the first flight of my life. The lieutenant took me through loops and rolls for about an hour to see my reaction and if I could handle flying. I handled it with ease; in fact, I loved it all. It was a great experience. What a ride!

The procedure to recover a plane from an ocean landing or one that has been involuntarily ditched was reasonably simple. After landing in the water, we taxied our way to the ship and then aligned ourselves as best we could with a large canvas net that was dropped into the water by a swing boom (a large crane).

Also attached to the swing boom were cables with metal hooks at their ends. Each hook was lowered to the plane and connected to an I-bolt that was a part of the aircraft's body. During my first flight, I had to stand up (while the pilot was holding my belt so I would not fall into the drink), grab the cable, and attach it to our plane. The plane, the pilot, and I were then hoisted up, and the aircraft was reattached to the catapult. I must say, the process from start to finish went like clockwork.

After that initial flight, I realized this was what I wanted to do. I wanted to fly planes. I was hooked. It was hard to return to my regular duties, and over the next few weeks, I could not imagine myself not being a naval aviator.

On October 22, 1941, we were on maneuvers with the other battleships. We had all been sailing in line, making turns in unison, when the USS *Oklahoma* rammed us. I was on duty on the bridge; it was not a big deal, just a wrong turn. The accident put a hole in the starboard side of the ship about thirty feet wide by eighteen to twenty feet high. We encountered a little bit of flooding, which caused us to list about ten degrees. We counter-flooded the other side of the ship, which set us up straight.

We immediately returned to Pearl Harbor and went to dry-dock. We were only in for five or six days for repairs, and that even included a new search radar that they installed atop the foremast. The damage to the USS *Arizona* was not extensive, and since we were scheduled to leave for the shipyard in Bremerton, Washington, in December, they probably did a rush job just to make sure we were seaworthy.

In November, I received a letter from Admiral Calhoun that I had been accepted into flight school and that he had approved the transfer. B. J. had also been taken. We were so excited; we were going to flight school, and we were going to be naval aviators. It was a great feeling.

I immediately shared the news with Hester and her parents. They were all sad that I was going to be leaving, but all of them, including Hester, wanted me to achieve the most success I could, so they were all encouraging and supportive.

The Hitchcocks were my family—my *ohana*. Having their support was important to me, and while I was disappointed to be leaving Hawaii and my second family, I knew going to flight school was the opportunity of a lifetime.

Flight school was in Pensacola, Florida, and initially the

Navy had booked our passage from Hawaii to California on the ocean liner SS *Lurline*, a cruise ship owned by the Matson Line that sailed from California (alternating between San Francisco and Los Angeles) to Honolulu. It was a first-class cruise ship that made the crossing in four and a half days. Passengers aboard the SS *Lurline* would spend nine days in Hawaii before returning to California.

A few days later, Captain Van Valkenburgh called us down and said, "Johnston, Conter, we're scheduled to leave for Long Beach in December to pick up our 1.1-inch quadruple machine-gun mounts. So even though you've been accepted to flight school, I'm not going to waste Navy money sending you back on the *Lurline*. You can wait and go back with us." We both responded with a resounding "yes, sir" and exited the captain's quarters.

It did not matter that we had to wait a few more weeks before leaving for flight school. We were still sky high. We were going to be naval aviators.

In late November, we were once again put out to sea and engaged in maneuvers. Then on December 4, 1941, we were involved in a night-firing exercise with Battleship Division One. It would be the last time the big guns of the USS *Arizona* would fire.

We were not scheduled to return to port until December 8, 1941, but we had received orders to return on December 5, 1941. I was the helmsman for the transit of the USS *Arizona* both in and out of Pearl Harbor on that trip, so, consequently, as were began heading into Pearl Harbor on December 5, I was on the bridge. Admiral Kidd and Captain Van Valkenburgh, standing a few feet away from me, engaged in a conversation, and I overheard Admiral Kidd tell Captain Van Valkenburgh that "we should not be going back into port, period." Neither was happy about returning to Pearl Harbor; my guess is if they had their druthers, we would have remained at sea.

As we approached the mooring quays near Ford Island, I guided the USS *Arizona* to a stop, and she was secured. Little did I know that she would remain moored in that exact spot for eternity.

The following day, Saturday, December 6, the USS *Vestal* (AR-4) pulled us together to conduct some minor maintenance and repair work. A little later in the morning, Admiral Kidd held a meeting with the other admirals and the captains under his command.

No one knew the nature of the meeting, but everyone knew the winds of war were blowing, and while we did not know when we were going to get involved in World War II, most of us knew American involvement in the war was coming; we just did not think it was coming with the next sunrise.

That evening, I stayed aboard the USS *Arizona*.

5

THE NIGHTMARE OF IT ALL

THE MORNING OF DECEMBER 7, 1941, was a normal workday for me. I was quartermaster of the watch on the quarterdeck that morning, so I was up early, had breakfast, and made my way topside at a quarter to eight or so.

That morning was beautiful. The weather observer at Hickam Field in Honolulu reported mainly clear skies each hour with mild temperatures and light east-to-northeast winds.

When I got to my duty station, which was toward the stern of the ship, I noticed that some of the ship's band was on the fantail preparing to play colors, which they always performed at exactly eight o'clock when we were in port. There was a Marine Color Guard in the area as well.

It was about 7:55 a.m. when the sound of the band tuning up gave way to the low whine of plane engines; the sound grew louder and louder as more and more planes began approaching Pearl Harbor. Everyone saw the red ball on the planes; it was the Japanese rising sun, and we all knew what was happening.

The first call was to close all watertight doors, and immediately thereafter we sounded general quarters. Within thirty seconds of seeing the first Japanese plane, the first guns were firing, and within two minutes, the five-inch antiaircraft guns were as well.

On deck, the band members had laid down their instruments, and, like everyone else, they rushed to their battle stations. For years, the newspapers said all the band members were in their bunks when the *Arizona* was attacked, and they all died in their sleep; well, that was a big lie. Many of them were on deck, and like every other sailor aboard ship, all of them were at their battleship stations within minutes of the attack.

The sky was filled with planes. The first wave of the Japanese attack consisted of 183 fighters, bombers, and torpedo planes, and they were swarming all about Pearl Harbor. There was machinegun fire, antiaircraft fire, and bombs seemingly exploding all around us.

It was my job to keep the log on everything that was happening. When Captain Van Valkenburgh entered the quartermaster office on his way to the bridge, he ordered Curtis Haynes, our other quartermaster, to grab the logbook and follow him; he ordered me to secure the quarterdeck and then head to the bridge. Admiral Kidd entered a few minutes later, and like Captain Van Valkenberg, he went to get the ship underway.

The USS *Vestal* was outboard of us and had to be cut loose. Aviation Machinist Mate First Class Donald Graham said, "Let's get at it," and the two of us went forward to cut the lines. We made our way along deck to cut the lines to the USS *Vestal,* and we also pulled in the gangplank so we could get the ship underway. Don was recognized for his efforts that day on December 7, 1998, Fifty-Seventh National Pearl Harbor Remembrance Day. Rear Admiral William G. Sutton, Commander, Naval Base Pearl Harbor, acknowledged Don's actions:

Aboard the Arizona, Aviation Machinist's Mate 1st Class Donald Graham braved intense flames and machine-gun fire, to release the lines connecting the battleship with the repair ship USS *Vestal*. Graham's actions allow the USS *Vestal* to get underway to safety. The Navy Cross is presented to Donald A. Graham, Aviation Machinist's Mate First Class, U.S. Navy, for exceptional courage, presence of mind, and devotion to duty and disregard for his personal safety while serving aboard the USS *Arizona* (BB-39) during the Japanese attack on the United States Pacific Fleet in Pearl Harbor, Territory of Hawaii, 7 December 1941. Although his shipmates were leaving the blazing USS *Arizona*, on his own initiative Aviation Machinist's Mate First Class Graham faced the intense fire on the deck, severe bombing and withering machine-gun fire of enemy strafing planes to release lines connecting the battleship with a repair vessel, USS *Vestal*, thus aiding the latter in getting underway. The conduct of Aviation Machinist's Mate First Class Graham throughout this action reflects great credit upon himself, and was in keeping with the highest traditions of the United States Naval Service (USSArizona.org, 2015).

Pearl Harbor was Don's second Navy Cross. He received his first in the Asiatic Theater aboard the gunboat the USS *Panay*; they were on the Yangtze River and under fire. He was a third-class boatswain mate and was manning a thirty-caliber gun.

The noise in Pearl Harbor was deafening. We were being bombed, torpedoed, and strafed. Most of our antiaircraft guns were in full action, and my shipmates manning these positions were performing their duties just as they had been trained to do. The Japanese planes approached the harbor, and their targets were clearly the battleships that were sitting along Ford Island. Seven battleships were in port on December 7, 1941; the USS *Arizona*, the USS *California*, the USS *Maryland*, the USS *Nevada*, the USS *Oklahoma*, the USS *Tennessee*, and the USS *West Virginia*; another, the USS *Pennsylvania,* was in drydock.

The Japanese assault was unrelenting as their fighters were buzzing the harbor on their strafing runs, and high-level bombers were dropping 1,760-pound armor-piercing projectiles from ten thousand feet above.

The first bomb to hit the *Arizona* bounced off the number four gun turret faceplate, went through the deck, and ended up exploding three decks down. Three or four other bombs missed us. Then the second bomb to hit did so on the portside somewhere near the antiaircraft deck; a third bomb struck the portside of the ship somewhere near the antitorpedo bulkhead. Even though the *Arizona* had taken three bomb hits, she was still in surprisingly good shape and prepping for getting underway. The *Vestal* took at least two bomb hits and looked as if she was in a little trouble.

Then, at about eight or nine minutes after eight o'clock, just thirteen minutes into the attack, the fourth bomb hit the *Arizona*. It was a lucky hit. The bomb penetrated the forward starboard deck in the number two turret about forty feet from the bow and passed through five steel decks before exploding near the forward lower handling room, which was my battle station when I first came aboard the *Arizona*. The bomb ignited over a million pounds of gunpowder and hundreds of thousands of pounds of ammunition.

I was between the quartermaster office and number-three turret at the base of the mainmast when the bomb, and all that powder, exploded. The sound of the blast was massive and unlike anything I had ever heard before or since. The bow of the ship, all thirty-four thousand tons, raised about thirty to forty feet out of the water, and, just as fast, settled down into the bottom of the channel. The ship was consumed in a giant fireball that looked as if it engulfed everything from the mainmast forward.

The explosion had gutted the forward decks. The turrets and the conning tower had dropped forty feet into the ship's hull, the forward mast had titled hard to her starboard side, the bow sagged where it split from the rest of the hull, and the *Arizona* was burning furiously. Fire and black smoke billowed hundreds of feet into the sky.

I never made it to the bridge.

Fourteen minutes after the first Japanese plane was spotted, the *Arizona* was dead, as were 1,177 of her crew. Those of us who had survived the explosion had no time to reflect or pause and give thought to what had just happened; rather, our job was to tend to the wounded.

Lieutenant Commander (LCDR) Samuel G. Fuqua, our senior surviving officer, had been knocked unconscious by the blast, regained consciousness, and made his way to the quarterdeck. Like so many other officers aboard the USS *Arizona*, LCDR Fuqua was a graduate of the US Naval Academy and had extensive experience aboard ships, with his very first duty being aboard the USS *Arizona* in 1923. After his first stint with the USS *Arizona*, LCDR Fuqua served on a number of ships and at several duty stations. He returned to the USS *Arizona* in the spring of 1941 as the ship's damage control officer after serving at the Naval Training Station, Great Lakes, Illinois, from 1939 to '41.

LCDR Fuqua immediately took charge and ordered all the able-bodied survivors to begin tending to the wounded, who, by that time, were pouring out of the forward part of the ship and onto the quarterdeck.

Men were emerging from the flames below; they were blinded, wounded, or literally burning. There were men who were fighting for their lives, fighting for survival. Some of them began jumping off the ship, but when they jumped in the water, they were basically jumping into a pool of burning fuel and oil.

LCDR Fuqua gave the order to physically restrain and even render our wounded shipmates unconscious if necessary to prevent them from jumping ship. As a man emerged from the smoke and flames, several of us would rush to help him; sadly, however, as we guided these men to safety, more often than not, their burned skin would come off in our hands. It was horrible . . . absolutely horrible.

The ship was burning out of control, so we had to organize teams to keep the flames away from the wounded (and the dead), who we had lying on the deck awaiting transport off ship. At one point, we had about fifteen men laid down on the deck. They were all in bad shape, and most were in a great deal of pain.

Even though the *Arizona* was ablaze, our guns were still firing at the enemy. We were tied up right alongside the quays, and there were several liberty launches that were tied up also. By then, lifeboats were also underway, and we began transporting the wounded from the bridge right onto the quays on the starboard side, where they were being taken to hospitals.

Only when LCDR Fuqua was satisfied that there were no remaining men aboard who were alive and that nothing more could be done for the USS *Arizona* did he give the order for all hands to abandon ship. The remaining injured were transferred to the admiral's barge, and we headed to the dock with the injured men.

After unloading the injured, I got into the number-two motor launch with several other survivors to begin a search for the wounded and any of the dead still in the water. The motor launches were fifty-foot boats that were quite maneuverable, making getting in and about the burning ships much more manageable than if we were to use the larger barges.

We rescued several survivors from the water, some still covered with burning oil, some trying to swim to Ford Island, which was not extremely far unless you were in water that was aflame with fuel and oil.

We used the motor launches to transport dozens of men to shore so they could be taken to the hospital. Some of them came from the water and some from the USS *Vestal*. Two of those men, Lauren Bruner and Don Stratton, became good friends of mine years later.

The second wave of Japanese planes reached Pearl Harbor at about 8:40 a.m. This assault consisted of 167 aircraft. There were no dive bombers or torpedo planes, and the high-level bombers concentrated their attacks on Ford Island, Kaneohe Naval Air Stations, and Hickam Field. However, the Japanese were unable to cause the level of destruction made by the first wave. This time, our defenses were much more organized, and we were more prepared.

The *Nevada*, which had sustained a torpedo hit during the first wave, had managed to get underway. Her chief quartermaster, Robert Sedberry, was guiding the ship to open waters when the Japanese attack group must have realized that if they sank her in the channel, it would close the harbor for months. The entire Japanese air fleet turned their attention to the *Nevada*. When Sedberry realized the ferocity of the attack and what the ramifications would be if the Japanese managed to sink the ship in the middle of the harbor, in a brilliant move, he decided to beach the *Nevada*. At first, the Navy was going to court-martial Sedberry, but smarter heads prevailed, and they ended up giving him the Medal of Honor for it.

During the second wave, rescue operations were in effect. There were so many men who were dead or dying, but one thing I want to make clear is that had it not been for the many selfless acts of bravery that had been taking place immediately after the first Japanese plane was spotted, more people would have lost their lives.

Shortly after 9:55 a.m., the Japanese withdrew. In the eight hours following the Pearl Harbor attack, Japan also attacked

British-held Singapore, Hong Kong, and Malaya and the US territorial possessions of the Philippines, Guam, and Wake Island.

Twenty-nine Japanese planes were lost in the attack on Oahu, nine during the first wave and twenty in the second wave; seventy-four were damaged by antiaircraft fire from the ground. Fifty-five Japanese airmen and nine submariners were killed in the attack, and one was captured.

Twenty-one ships of the US Pacific Fleet were sunk or damaged. Aircraft losses were 188 destroyed and 159 damaged. There was a total of 2,403 American casualties, including sixty-eight civilians, and there were 1,178 military and civilian wounded.

In his official report, LCDR Fuqua stated he could not single out any one individual who stood out in acts of heroism above the others as all the personnel conducted themselves with the greatest heroism and bravery. LCDR Fuqua was right. On December 7, 1941, there were many who showed tremendous courage in the face of grave danger, and there were many whose efforts that day went above and beyond the call of duty.

At no time were our military forces reduced to a confused rabble as some sensational reports would have you believe. All the military people performed admirably under extremely difficult circumstances.

Many leading questions have been asked about the Pearl Harbor attack. Yes, some links were missing; command relations and responsibilities were not clearly established. Communications were not what they should have been. Washington was lax with its help and information to the Pacific Fleet and US Army commands. However, the fighting units were well organized and disciplined.

The USS Arizona—my home space—was well organized and disciplined. We had been operating at sea for many months since April 1940 under realistic wartime conditions. The crew could handle any emergency.

The USS Arizona is probably better known today than during

her twenty-five-year life in the US Fleet. Millions of people have visited the memorial. She was a great ship on December 7, 1941. She is a great ship today. A ship with a confident captain and crew will always remain a good ship. Our captain is still aboard.

We had thirty-six sets of brothers and one father and son. Of the brothers, three were sets of three brothers. Only one set survived.

To bring up a little-known fact of history, the five Sullivan brothers from Waterloo, Iowa, who died aboard the USS *Juneau* on November 13, 1942, comprised the greatest loss of any one family in US naval history. The irony of this is that the Sullivan brothers joined the Navy to avenge the death of a very good friend, Bill Ball of Fredericksburg, Iowa, who was killed aboard the USS *Arizona* on December 7, 1941.

I was one of only 335 sailors, and one of thirty-four quartermasters, who survived the attack on the USS *Arizona*. The ship lost 1,177 souls.

A few months after the attack on Pearl Harbor, I was honored with a commendation for my actions. The notation placed in my service jacket read as follows:

Commended by Commanding Officer USS ARIZONA for distinguished conduct during the Japanese attack on Pearl Harbor, T. H., on 7 December 1941 in which that vessel was destroyed. His heroism in fighting his ship and assisting wounded men to abandon ship and devotion to duty after the attack through assisting and volunteering for various details such as firefighting and watch standing was in keeping with the highest tradition of the Naval Service. Is entitled to the Asiatic-Pacific Area Campaign Medal with bronze star. Authorized to wear Asiatic-Pacific Service Ribbon with bronze star.

—Captain Ellis Hugh Geiselman

To this day, I am proud of my actions that I engaged in during and after the attack on Pearl Harbor. I am proud of all the men who were serving aboard the USS *Arizona* on that day of infamy.

Since 1991 (the fiftieth anniversary of the attack), I have attended the Pearl Harbor Remembrance Ceremony. I am blessed to have family and friends who go with me every December 7 so I can pay tribute to those who lost their lives during the attack. When I first go aboard the ship, I make my way through the entry and the assembly room as quickly as I can and go directly to the shrine room. After I enter the shrine room, I always have to take a breath. It is still a shock to walk into that room and see the names of the men etched on that marble wall. I look at the wall for a few moments and then look to the names of those survivors who have been interned in the years since that faithful day. I say a prayer for my lost brothers and salute them. That moment is tough. But you take a breath, say a prayer, and thank God you are alive.

6

Life after the
Day of Infamy

THE SECOND WAVE OF Japanese planes left Oahu a little before
10:00 a.m. We had no idea if there was going to be another
attack, an invasion, or what. One thing we did know was that
we had injured people who needed medical care. Also, the lower
handling rooms of turrets three and four still had about one million pounds of powder that could have exploded at any time, so
trying to get the fires under control was a big priority.

There were many dead, dying, and wounded Sailors and Marines lying on the ground on Ford Island; it was a god-awful
sight. The injured were being sent to a variety of medical facilities. The Naval Hospital Pearl Harbor, which was the largest
facility available, was receiving the bulk of the wounded. The
medical personnel was able to activate a makeshift field hospital
at the Officer's Club located on the Navy yard. The USS *Solace*,
which lay anchor off Battleship Row at Ford Island, and the USS
Argonne also handled many of the injured.

When we returned to the USS *Arizona* to battle the fire, it
was blazing furiously. It was an inferno. Columns of thick black

smoke with reddish-orange flames filled the deep-blue sky. It was hard to breathe and even see at times.

Jay Blount, a spokesman for the Pearl Harbor National Memorial, was once quoted as saying, "The USS *Arizona* burned for two and a half days after the initial attack; temperatures reached as high as 8000°F, which is more than three times as hot as lava spurting out of Hawaii's Kilauea volcano."

Most of us fought the fire on the USS *Arizona* for forty-eight hours straight and worked into Tuesday night, December 9, 1941. After we were relieved of duty on Tuesday evening, I returned to base, where I crapped out for over twelve hours.

It took the ship about five days to cool down.

Under the lead of Water Tender First Class (WT 1/C) Pete Hozar, the number-one diver aboard the USS *Arizona*, I was assigned to dive on the ship to look for survivors or records and to claim any bodies.

There were about ten to fifteen of us who were outfitted with shallow water helmets. They were simple cast bronze helmets placed over our heads that rested on our shoulders. The air was supplied through an air hose that attached to the helmet. A man topside pumped air into the hose. On average, we could stay down for about twenty to forty minutes.

I remember my first dive; we found about five bodies in the officers' quarters. It was a tough job. We would have to get the air out of the bodies before sending them topside, where they were cared for on a platform that had been set up.

We worked the detail for several days before the Navy decided it was too dangerous to continue the operation. Not only were the air hoses of the divers getting caught on the jagged edges of the ruptured hatches, but there were some growing concerns about all the unexploded powder and ammunition that was still aboard the ship.

My time as a sailor aboard the USS *Arizona* was officially over.

All those who survived the attack were assigned to other ships or commands needing manpower. I was assigned to Commander Base Force tugboats delivering supplies to Kauai, and B. J. Johnston, who was assigned to Division 5 AA on the gun deck of the USS *Arizona,* was sent to a destroyer for duty.

Immediately after the attack on Pearl Harbor, Hawaii's territorial governor, Joseph B. Poindexter, declared martial law. The military ordered a complete blackout. Saloons were closed, the sale of liquor was prohibited, schools were closed, gasoline rationing went into effect, and even food sales were suspended. Martial law had to go in effect since we did not know what we were dealing with. There were rumors that the air attack was just the beginning of a full-scale invasion of Oahu by the Japanese, so the order was given that no one could go out after sunset or before sunrise, or they would get shot.

Commander Geiselman, USS *Arizona's* executive officer, was ashore with his family on December 7. Following the sinking of the USS *Arizona,* Commander Geiselman reported the next day for duty as senior naval representative on the staff of the military governor of the Hawaiian Islands, when the islands were placed under military government. After the commander of the Pacific told his skippers to send their most experienced and trusted men to shore-patrol duty, Commander Geiselman assigned me and Pete Hozar, a water tender first class (WT 1st), who was also a member of the football team, to Pearl Harbor Base Force.

Before the war started, I was assigned to shore patrol while the USS *Arizona* was in port. Shore patrol then was not like it is today. The guys back then were not military police. We had some basic training and nothing else. I was on the USS *Arizona's* pistol team in 1940, and we used to go to Barber's Point when we were in port. I could hit a target at one hundred feet, which is not easy to do with a .45-caliber handgun. I guess that made me more qualified than most guys.

In the weeks after December 7, the guys were getting a little rowdy, especially on Hotel Street. Commander Geiselman was tasked with keeping the peace. He knew that I had experience working shore patrol on Hotel Street before the war, so Pete and I were assigned the duty. We worked with the local police to help get things squared away.

During my pre-December 7 shore-patrol duties, I had developed a relationship with several of the girls and the madams who worked in the brothels. It was all strictly business, no hanky-panky, but I will admit there were times when I sat with the madams and enjoyed a cup of coffee.

Hotel Street and the side streets branching off it probably had close to twenty brothels. The boogie houses, as they were called, ended up being one of the most fruitful entrepreneurial businesses in Hawaii.

Immediately after the attack on Oahu, many of the brothels served as quarters for the wounded. Several months later, the military ended up getting somewhat involved in the quasi-legal prostitution business by setting a price limit of three dollars per visit so that visiting sailors would not lose all their money.

Whenever ships came into Pearl Harbor, hundreds of men would be outside the brothels waiting to get inside. To satisfy the immense demand for female companionship, men were kept in a bullpen of three or more rooms, which permitted them to dress and undress in assembly-line fashion, while each received only three minutes of "personal attention" (Bailey & Farber, 1992).

By switching from room to room, a prostitute could see as many as one hundred customers a day. She kept two out of each three dollars she was paid and gave the madam one. Clients entered the hotel, paid three dollars for a poker chip, and were taken to a room to undress. The prostitute came into the room, collected the poker chip, and manually inspected the man for venereal disease before washing him. He was given three minutes to do his business before being whisked off into another room to wash and get dressed (Fawcett, 2015).

Our job was to keep the peace, and by the time a sailor was ready to visit one of the establishments on Hotel Street, he was usually no longer in the mood for fighting.

Hotel Street was also lined with bars. This was where things usually got a little more rambunctious. Still, it was sailors and marines just blowing off some steam. If guys did not comply with the rules and guidelines in place, they were placed on report, and there was always hell to pay when they returned to their ships.

No one wanted to lose their liberty privileges, so for the most part, the problems we encountered were minor.

Each battleship had a preferred bar or watering hole, as they were called. The USS *Nevada* crewmen laid claim to Shanghai Bill's Bar, the USS *Maryland* guys were frequent visitors of the Four Aces Bar, and my shipmates from the USS *Arizona* called Smith's Union Bar their home.

Smiths, or Smitty's, was established in 1934 and can now lay claim to being the oldest bar on the island. The bar was run by Joe Holley and later by his son, Leroy. Joe was a military man who served in the Army during World War I. After the war, he married, settled in Oahu, and opened Smiths.

I never frequented Smitty's when I was a member of the USS *Arizona;* I was either working or studying, but many of my crewmates did. I did, however, visit Smitty's many years later.

As I said, the island was under martial law; there were no public hearings, and the decree was enforced at the point of a bayonet. No one was allowed out after dark or before daylight. Anyone seen on the streets faced the real threat of being shot.

Martial law worked exactly as it was supposed to work. The only rules on the beach were common sense; if a police officer or military officer told you to do something, you did it—no questions asked, no arguments.

We did not have cell phones in 1941, nor did we have open access to phones, period. I knew that my parents, like so many of the parents with sons or daughters in Hawaii during the attack on Pearl Harbor, were probably worried sick since they had not heard from me. On Saturday, December 14, 1941, I saw Hester for a moment, and she told me her father would be in his office to check on his crews.

I went to Mr. Hitchcock's office and was able to call home and let everyone know I was okay. It was a short call, about thirty seconds, but my folks had peace of mind knowing that I was alive. Then, on December 20, 1941, my mother received a telegram from the government that read:

> The Navy Department deeply regrets to inform you that your son Louis Anthony Counter (Conter) quartermaster third class US Navy is missing following action in the performance of his duty and in the service of his country. The department appreciates your great anxiety and will furnish you with further information promptly when received. To prevent possible aid to our enemies, please do not divulge the name of his ship or station.
> —Rear Admiral Randall Jacob, Chief of the Bureau of Navigation.

Once again, my mother was left wondering if I had been reassigned and was now missing in action. It was a terrible time. I had no idea she had received the telegram, so as far as I was concerned, my parents thought I was okay.

On January 8, 1942, I received my first liberty. I went to Hester's house for dinner, and Admiral Calhoun walked in.

He looked at me and said, "Conter, I thought I sent you to flight school." I said, "Captain Van Valkenburg had decided to wait on our transfer until the USS *Arizona* reported stateside, and then our orders were lost on the USS *Arizona* on December seventh, sir." He nodded his head and said, "I'll take care of it," and he did; three days later, both B. J. and I had orders to report to the SS *Lurline* for passage to San Francisco.

I called my folks to give them the news that I would be heading to flight school and stopping by the house while on leave. They thought I was missing because of some other attack or mission. Luckily, I was fine, and I think my parents were just relieved (again) that I was okay. When my mother heard I was going to be a pilot, she said, "Oh, you're really gonna get killed now."

The SS *Lurline*, a steamship, was a Matson Lines vessel and was halfway from Honolulu to San Francisco on December 7, 1941, when the Japanese bombed Pearl Harbor. They rushed like crazy to get to California. After it was deemed safe, the SS *Lurline*, with her Matson sister ships the SS *Mariposa* and SS *Monterey*, returned to Hawaii to help transport troops and supplies to Hawaii.

When B. J. and I stepped aboard the SS *Lurline*, we found the ship loaded with approximately fourteen hundred people. Injured military members and civilians made up the bulk of the travelers, but the SS *Lurline* was also carrying Navy spouses, their children, and other civilians who were simply caught on the island during the attack and needed to get home.

The skipper of the ship called us to his cabin and said, "You're in the Navy; you know what's happening, and you know what to do. So your job is to keep everyone safe."

It was a shaky trip. There were a lot of burn victims. The wives and children were somewhat upset, as you could imagine, and the seas, which can be unkind at times, were pretty rough.

Six days after we left Hawaii, we docked in San Francisco, California. We had some leave coming to us, so B. J. and I both headed home for a few days. B. J. went to Texas, and I went to Colorado to visit my folks. After spending a few days in Denver, I took the train to Kentucky to visit my sister Mary. She was attending Loretta Heights College and was studying to be a nun. It was great seeing Mary; she was doing well, and she had found her calling. After my visit with Mary, I left for Pensacola.

Back in the '40s, the trains had bunks for passengers to sleep. In many ways, it was an upgrade to the hammocks we had aboard ship. I did not mind traveling by train; in fact, I found it to be a very pleasurable experience.

7

FLIGHT SCHOOL

I ARRIVED IN PENSACOLA, Florida, and began my flight training on January 20, 1942. For those of you who don't know a great deal about Pensacola, it has a fascinating history. There has been a military presence in the Pensacola area since the Spanish tried to establish a colony there in 1559. That effort failed after a few years, but in the late seventeenth century, the Spanish returned to the natural deep-water port to build forts to defend the western part of their Florida colony (The Florida Historical Society, 2020).

Through the nineteenth century, the US government built forts on the barrier islands and the mainland and early in the twentieth century began development of two major enterprises, ship building and aviation, the latter of which remains the major activity there to this day (The Florida Historical Society, 2020).

The Florida Historical Society Library houses a collection of photographs taken by civilian shipwright B. E. Williams, who worked at the Pensacola Ship Building Company before and during the First World War. This includes photos of major events, such as the March 1917 launch of the *Cushnoc*, the first boat built at the Pensacola shipyard (The Florida Historical Society, 2020).

Pensacola began as a Navy yard and was one of the best-equipped naval stations in the country. In its early years, the primary mission of the base was to facilitate missions designated to suppress the slave trade and piracy in the Gulf of Mexico and Caribbean Sea (Naval History and Heritage Command, 2020).

The Navy Department, awakened to the possibilities of aviation, began prevailing upon Congress to include a provision for aeronautical development in the Naval Appropriation Act enacted in 1911–12. In October 1913, Secretary of the Navy Josephus Daniels appointed a board to make a survey of aeronautical needs and establish a policy to guide future development. One of the board's most important recommendations was the establishment of an aviation training station in Pensacola (Naval History and Heritage Command, 2020).

Upon entry into World War I, Pensacola, still the only naval air station in the United States, had thirty-eight naval aviators, 163 enlisted men trained in aviation, and fifty-four airplanes. Two years later, by the signing of the armistice in November 1918, the air station, with 438 officers and 5,538 enlisted men, had trained one thousand naval aviators. At the war's end, seaplanes, dirigibles, and free kite balloons were housed in steel and wooden hangars stretching a mile down the air station beach (Naval History and Heritage Command, 2020).

In the years following World War I, aviation training slowed down. An average of one hundred pilots were graduating yearly from the twelve-month flight course. This was before the days of aviation cadets, and the majority of the students included in the flight training program were Annapolis graduates. A few enlisted men also graduated. Thus, Naval Air Station Pensacola became known as the Annapolis of the Air (Naval History and Heritage Command, 2020).

With the inauguration in 1935 of the cadet training program, activity at Pensacola again expanded. When Pensacola's training facilities could no longer accommodate the ever-increasing number of cadets accepted by the Navy, two more naval air stations were created—one in Jacksonville, Florida, and the other in Corpus Christi, Texas. In August 1940, a larger auxiliary base, Saufley Field, was added to Pensacola's activities. In October 1941, a third base, Ellyson Field, was commissioned. During World War II, NAS Pensacola once again became the hub of air training activities. The air station expanded again, training up to eleven hundred cadets a month, eleven times the amount trained annually in the 1920s (Naval History and Heritage Command, 2020).

I arrived at NAS Pensacola, Florida, toward the end of January. I was one of thirty in my class, and our class was the last one that month. We had a pretty diversified group of rates. As one would expect, the aviation rates were well represented as we had guys who were aviation machinists, electricians, boatswains, aerographers, and riggers, but several of us were not from the aviation family, including me and B. J.

We were busy during flight school. The days were long, and we were working seven-day weeks. I couldn't tell you much about Pensacola, Florida, other than what it looked like from the air simply because we had zero free time to get out and about, which was okay with me because I was there to become an aviator.

We spent the first few weeks of flight school doing all our groundwork and getting acquainted with all things aviation. We learned about every element involved in an airplane: drag, lift, airspeed, stalling, and spins. We learned about engines—what made them tick and how to perform maintenance on them. We learned to recognize every ship on the sea and every plane in the air.

We had PT every day, during which we marched and did exercises that consisted of sit-ups and push-ups. We also did sea survival in the pool. We were taught how to inflate a raft and get it turned over (which is not that easy when you are treading water), and we learned how to float. The sea survival instruction sure came in handy for many of us—as we would come to learn several months later.

During our first thirty days, we had two days of water training and two or three classes on survival, and then we were sent to New Orleans, Louisiana, to do our basic flight training.

As I have mentioned, we had a good mix of rates in our class, so we helped each other when it came to studying for our exams. The aviation guys helped with the aviation aspects of our studies, and since I was a quartermaster, I helped everyone with the navigation side of things. We all worked together as a team, and as a result, we all passed our tests.

We spent three weeks in New Orleans and did our first forty hours of flight training while we were in Louisiana. We flew for most of the days and into the nights. It was a great experience.

My first flight was in an N3N Navy Trainer, a tandem-seat, open-cockpit, and primary training biplane aircraft. I sat in the front of the plane; my instructor sat in the back and gave me orders through a speaking tube. We spent the bulk of our hours in the N3N Navy Trainer, although we worked in a few other types of planes as well.

We did our aerobatics, snap rolls, and loops, and I took my first solo flight in the N3N Navy Trainer; she was an excellent aircraft. The solo flight was a simple and relatively brief experience. I taxied down to the end of the runway. When I was clear and ready to go, I gave it the throttle and started to move down the runway quickly. It did not take long to get enough speed to lift off. During that first flight, I did not go very high, nor did I go very far; I just took off, circled the field a few times, and then landed. But in that short period of time, I was hooked.

As I was flying on that first flight, I thought back to when I was a kid and how I had never thought about flying. I never even imagined I would have the opportunity to do it. It was an exhilarating experience. While I was concentrating on the physical part of flying, I still had the opportunity to look around and see the whole horizon and everything below. It was like nothing I ever imagined. It was great being by myself; it made me think, *How did I even do this?* I felt a sense of accomplishment; I was one of a select few. There were only about one thousand Navy aviation pilots at that time, and I was one of them.

When we returned to Pensacola, I was assigned to Squadron 4, and that was when our training really began. I received training on instruments in SNJs, and I received formation flying in SNCs. For anyone wondering, SNJ stands for scout (S), trainer (N), and the J was the location, North America; SNC stands for scout, trainer, and the C was for the builder, Curtiss.

The classes for instrument flying were conducted with the SNJ Squadron. We had already soloed and had forty to fifty hours of flying before and had some instrument training already. So our training was basically sitting in a Link Trainer and making sure we knew all the intimate details of how to operate the various instruments.

One of the things we learned was how to land using the needle/ball/airspeed method, which was a 1-2-3 system for aircraft control. This system was based on three successive steps: (1) center the turn needle using the rudder, (2) center the ball with *aileron* control, and (3) control the airspeed with the elevator (Soekkha, 1997). In other words, we had to use our instruments and keep our eyes moving while reading all three gauges.

Keep in mind that there was no radar, nor did we have all of the onboard computers or equipment that today's aviators have, so being able to read our instruments was the only means of flying that we had available.

After instrument training, we moved to formation flying. From the early days of naval aviation, formation flying has been instrumental in the tactical movement of aircraft. Whether you are a wingman on a cross-country flight or the lead on a multi-plane combat strike against an enemy stronghold, good formation flying is critical to the success of the mission. Because flying in formation is a team effort, the success of the flight depends on individual efforts coordinated with other flight members (Department of the Navy, 2020). Flying in formation was also used to prepare us for carrier duty, but the primary reason for learning how to fly in formation back in the 1940s was so we could stay in visual contact with each other. The squadron leader was at the point, and that man was our eyes in the sky. He would be the one charged with returning us home.

We also trained in a pressure chamber, or altitude chamber, as some people called it. The pressure chamber is used to simulate the effects of high altitude on the human body, especially hypoxia (low oxygen) and hypobaria (low ambient air pressure). After some classroom training, we entered the chamber, where the training began. During the instructional phase of the training, the emphasis was placed on not taking off our masks. We were told to breathe oxygen to purge nitrogen from the bloodstream so decompression sickness wouldn't occur. The chamber simulated up to thirty thousand feet, which was way over what we needed. Our planes only flew about twelve thousand feet, so our training more than covered the actual events that we would encounter as pilots.

I did not have any ill effects from the training; a few of the others may have had a side effect or two, but for the most part, the entire class did just fine. I kept my mask on, and just like with our formation flying, none of us had any serious issues, and no one passed out.

One of the final elements of my basic flight school training was learning how to conduct a dive-bombing run. During dive-bombing training, we went up with four planes, flying in formation, and aimed at the targets that were previously set up on land and in the water. The land targets were big squares with flags tied to them, and the water targets were tied to wood floats. For the land targets, we would drop from about ten thousand feet and dry bomb them. We were at about twenty-five hundred feet over the water targets. We trained for about twenty to thirty hours, practicing for air-to-land attacks and attacks on aircraft, cruisers, and battleships.

After all of the basic flight training, I began PBY training with Squadron 4 in Pensacola. Except for the PBY 5A, all of the PBYs were water-based, meaning they took off and landed on the water, so my training focused on the twin-engine PBYs' water landings, especially rough-water landings.

I'll talk in more detail about the PBY in the next chapter, but just for some brief background information, the designation "PBY" was determined in accordance with the US Navy aircraft designation system of 1922, with PB representing "patrol bomber" and Y being the manufacturer code assigned to Consolidated Aircraft. I started in a PB2Y Coronado, a large flying boat patrol bomber designed by Consolidated Aircraft and used by the US Navy during World War II in bombing, anti-submarining, and transporting roles.

I was then placed with Squadron 5, where I received training in the PBY. We practiced landing on runways in the PBY 5A since it was the only one with wheels. The wheel system weighed about three thousand pounds, so we did not use them for bombing; you couldn't put enough bombs on them because of the wheel weight. The PBY 5 had a range of nearly twenty-five hundred miles and was primarily used for search-and-rescue missions, but it was also used in long-range reconnaissance and did antisubmarine patrols. We also did night torpedo runs on the Japanese fleet.

I completed my PBY training, and I graduated from flight

school on November 15, 1942. I was ordered to VP-11 and was off to San Diego, California. Even though I still held the rank of quartermaster third class, I was a naval aviator.

As for my friend B. J., he was ordered to serve in a VJ squadron, which was a support group that dealt with serving with liaison activities (reconnaissance) and logistics. Sadly, B. J. and I lost touch after we completed flight school, and we never had contact again. I would learn years later that he ended up having a long and successful career in the Navy and, like me, retired as a lieutenant commander. He passed away on July 25, 1988, and was laid to rest in the Houston National Cemetery in Houston, Texas.

8

BLACK CAT SQUADRON

IN JUNE OF 1941, Congress passed Public Law 99, which specifically authorized the creation of a wartime enlisted pilot training program. Over the years, as many as five thousand enlisted men may have served as pilots with the Navy, Marine, and Coast Guard (Boyne, 2002), and I can say without reservation that I am very grateful to have been one of those men. Although I still held the rank of quartermaster third class (I would not receive my naval aviation pilot rating until 1943), I was still an aviator, and I was excited to start my new career.

When I graduated from flight school in November 1942, I was assigned to VP (Patrol Squadron 11), which meant I would be flying a PBY. Painted black, to prevent it from being easily seen by the Japanese, the PBY Black Cats had been designed to serve as a long-range search-and-rescue plane and patrol bomber and attack enemy transport ships at sea to disrupt enemy supply lines.

Many aviation experts considered the PBY Catalina obsolete when the war started, but combat proved the critics wrong. The "Cat" had two noteworthy attributes that made the airplane prized by American aviators and the flight crews of other Allied nations: great range and excellent durability. By VJ Day, August

15, 1945, Consolidated and its licensees had built 3,282 PBYs, more than any flying boat or seaplane ever built (Smithsonian National Air and Space Museum, 2020).

On the morning of December 7, 1941, during the attack on Pearl Harbor, most of the PBY squadron's aircraft were destroyed as they sat on the runways at Naval Air Station Kaneohe. There were thirty-six patrol planes at Kaneohe Air Station, thirty-three at Pearl Harbor, and twelve at Midway (Trojan, 2020).

Twelve of the patrol planes at Pearl Harbor had just returned on December 5 after completing an extensive tour of duty at Midway and Wake Islands and required much-needed maintenance. Patrol Squadron 11 had a total of twelve aircraft assigned to them; all their aircraft were parked at NAS Kaneohe Bay on the morning of December 7, 1941 (Trojan, 2020).

By April 1942, the squadron started to see replacement planes arrive. By July of that year, VP-11 deployed to Suva, Fiji Islands, and over the next several months, the squadron would be moved from Suva to Noumea, New Caledonia, Tongatabu, and Espiritu Santo to conduct search and reconnaissance missions in connection with the landings at Guadalcanal and other fleet operations in the South Pacific (Roberts, 2000).

Interestingly, the PBY Catalina Patrol Bombers were slated to be removed from service. Then the war broke out, and America needed every serviceable plane available. Someone figured out that if the PBYs were painted with a flat-black paint, the outdated aircraft might just make a formidable attack plane, and they were right.

The PBY was a tremendous plane. It could defy the most intolerable weather and the most tenacious enemy. The aircraft could bomb, strafe, and torpedo enemy submarine, surface warships, freighters, and troopships, and it was a deadly nuisance to the enemy in every naval war zone of the world. The planes patrolled thousands of miles of the world's oceans and seas, supporting allied fleets and merchant vessel movements. They battled the faster, better-armed, and more maneuverable German and Japanese aircraft.

For thousands of men and women throughout the world, the slow, clumsy-looking, amphibious seaplane became a mechanical angel of mercy. Braving impossible seas and often a hostile enemy, the Catalina PBYs rescued airmen, seamen, merchant mariners, refugees, Coastwatchers, and even the enemy. Little wonder that this angel of mercy became affectionately known as the Beloved Cat.

After spending ten days in Colorado with my folks, I headed to California and arrived in North Island (San Diego) in December of 1942. Most of the members of VP-11 had returned to California during the holidays for a refit on the planes and to give some of the unit's pilots and crew members some much-earned home leave.

In February 1943, we left San Diego for Hawaii. There were twelve PBY Black Cats in our squadron, and it took us nineteen hours and dozens of extra fuel cans to make the long flight. Upon arrival in Kaneohe, Hawaii, all hands undertook intensive combat preparation while simultaneously conducting patrols over the ocean in the Hawaiian area. We were also making runs back and forth to Midway Island.

During our time in Kaneohe, one of our assignments was to help new US Army Air Corp pilots learn flight navigation over water and how to make the necessary inflight navigational adjustments in response to environmental influences on the aircraft.

Many of the Air Corp pilots we worked with were on anti-submarine duty between Pearl Harbor and Midway. While some of them were resentful of us at first (after all, they were the seasoned veterans), they came to appreciate our navigational skills and were grateful for the things we were able to teach them.

In late May of 1943, I completed our combat training at Kaneohe and received my orders to go to Perth, Australia. The trip to Australia was nearly sixty-eight hundred miles, and it took us six days of flying nine hours per day. We arrived on June 8, 1943.

For almost two months, missions were flown between our base in Australia and the Timor and Philippine Islands. The bulk of our missions were combat search and reconnaissance patrols in the southwest Pacific. We were under the operational control of FAW-10.

A short while later, we were ordered to Port Moresby. We worked out of Jenkins Bay, near Samaria, British New Guinea. Our crews were based on tender ships moored in secluded harbors, and since our planes took off and landed on the water, we tied up to buoys near the USS *San Pablo* and the USS *Half Moon*, which were service ships for the PBYs.

The Fifth Bombardment Group of the US Army Air Force (USAAF) was at Port Moresby under the command of General George Kenney. Kenney had only been in charge of the group since July of 1942 after he received orders to take over the Allied Air Forces and Fifth Air Force in General Douglas MacArthur's Southwest Pacific Area. MacArthur had been dissatisfied with the performance of his air commander, Lieutenant General George Brett, and was offered a choice between Kenney and Major General James Doolittle. MacArthur chose Kenney (Wolk, 1987).

The USAAF handled the daytime attacks while conducting night searches for surface ships and bombing Japanese installations on Garove Island. We flew night missions to disrupt the Japanese-held locations and shipping lanes. We used a combination of ordnance, including torpedoes and bombs, and I have to say that our missions were highly successful. Our reconnaissance flights were able to give us a pretty accurate account of the routines of the Japanese ships, and we learned that the best time for a bombing raid was after 1:00 a.m., when the ship was quiet.

All PBYs carried parachute flares aboard the aircraft, and each plane carried between twelve and fourteen of these parachute flares on every mission. The flares, which had up to half a million candlepower, were set to go off at four thousand feet and would light up a Japanese location like it was the middle of the day. The PBY crews used parachute flares to keep hostile troops awake when an Allied morning attack was pending. This would increase the enemy's fatigue when the Allies launched their attack; it was a highly effective tactic. We would go into the Japanese lines and push out a parachute flare, and it would light up the entire area and keep the Japanese awake. We did this for a few weeks at a time. The Japanese would become exhausted, and it provided our daytime planes, the B-25s and B-17s, and the Navy planes taking off from the ships a little bit of an advantage.

Attacking in the middle of the night ensured that we would not get much fire back, and by the time they sounded general quarters, we were already on our way in for our runs. Sometimes they would start shooting at you, and you would look at the shells, and they looked like they were going to hit you. Then they would go by.

Our squadron would leave at five-thirty in the evening, stay out for twelve or fourteen hours, and then return in the morning. We would come back from our mission, eat, and then find a place on the beach to sleep. We would get a few days off and then repeat the cycle. The attacks were amazingly effective, and we knew we were starting to wear on the Japanese forces in the area.

9

SHOT DOWN . . . TWICE

DURING THAT LAST WEEK in September 1943, our plane was
on a run about seven miles off the coast of New Guinea when
a well-placed enemy round penetrated our aircraft through the
waste hatch and hit one of the parachute flares on the aft portion of the aircraft. A fire quickly spread to all the other parachute flares, and soon the plane was engulfed by the fire, so we
were forced to make an emergency landing in the ocean.

Everyone made it to the front of the plane, and we closed
the hatches to prevent the fire from spreading into the cockpit.
As soon as we hit the water, the crew evacuated through the pilot's escape hatch. The ocean was rough that night, with ten- to
fifteen-foot swells.

We had just taken off about two hours earlier, so we still had
two thousand-pound bombs and two five-hundred-pound bombs
under the wings of the plane; we were still carrying approximately seventeen hundred gallons of fuel. We were concerned that
the plane would explode, so we did not have a chance to grab
any rescue gear, not a single life jacket, no life rafts or boats.

We were all treading water in a pretty tight circle when Gordon Kennington, a lieutenant commander and our pilot, told
us, "Say your prayers, men; it's going to be dark soon. We've

got sharks all around us, we're about seven miles offshore, and I don't think any of us can swim that far in these fifteen-foot swells."

I replied, "Baloney. Knock it off. Just stay together, hold hands, and kick slowly. Yes, there are sharks around, but if a shark comes too close, hit it in the nose with your fist as hard as you can."

We had three officers aboard the plane and in the water with us, so I should not have said anything since I was just a first-class petty officer, but no one else said a word at a time when someone needed to speak up. We got the men to circle up, hold hands, and tread lightly in the water. The guys helped one another, and when someone weakened, someone would step up and help that person out.

The sharks did come, but just as I said, as soon as we hit one of them in the nose, it would turn the other way and swim away really fast. We were fortunate with sharks; there were other pilots and ship crew members who did not fare as well as we did in encounters with them.

We caught another break when our skipper, who was in the lead plane, noticed the fire from our aircraft and returned to look for survivors. He saw we were in the water without any life jackets or lifeboats, so he dropped one of his plane's lifeboats.

So I swam over, grabbed the lifeboat, and even though I could never turn a lifeboat over at Pensacola during survival training, I grabbed the cord to inflate the boat, gave it a yank, and the boat inflated. I flipped it over on the very first attempt. After I dove into the boat, I thought to myself, *How in the hell did I get in here?*

I paddled back to the men; we got everyone aboard and made our way to shore. We got into New Guinea at two-thirty or three o'clock in the morning. We got all the guys hidden in the jungle, and I told all of them to stay quiet. Do not fart because the Japanese would be out looking for us.

The jungle was only about one hundred feet from the water, but it was so dense that no one would find us unless they accidentally tripped over us. We were there for the rest of that night and the next day.

One of my crewmates and I watched the trails for patrols and made sure everyone was staying put and not getting overly anxious. That night, a little after midnight, we heard a familiar noise: the sound of a patrol torpedo (PT) boat, which is a motor torpedo boat that was small, maneuverable, and very fast.

I knew they would be looking for us. I told everyone to stay put, and we I would go check things out and come back for them if the sounds were from friendly forces, as we expected. I broke away from the jungle and got about one hundred feet from the boat before noticing the men on the PT boat had their machine-guns pointed at us. I told them to turn those goddamned machine-guns away. Then someone on the deck said, "That's Conter." They yelled at me, "Come on aboard!"

I swam out to the PT boat. After we boarded, I told them I had to go back and pick up the other guys; they were hidden in certain spots in the jungle, and they had been instructed to stay quiet and not answer anyone. The commander of the PT said, "No, you're staying here." The ship had three underwater demolition team (UDT) members with them; these were basically what are known today as Navy SEALs.

I gave the UDT men a briefing on all of our guys, where they were, their names, and even their hometowns back in the States. The three UDT members took off, and within forty-five minutes, they were back with every single man.

Upon coming aboard, each of the guys dropped to his knees and kissed the deck. They were so happy to be safely aboard the PT boat. Once everyone was secured, the skipper of the boat punched the throttle. The engines roared like a bomb had gone off, and we hightailed it out of there.

The next morning, we made it back to the tenders, where we were debriefed, had breakfast, and rested for most of the day. At five-thirty the next evening, we were given another PBY and made a 13.5-hour trip to Rabaul, New Guinea, where we engaged in our next mission: a dive-bombing run.

Years later, Lt. Commander Kennington's daughter, Joan, who was born in 1947, shared with my family that "without Lou saving my dad's life, I would have never been born." Gordon lived a long life and passed away on June 3, 2014, at the age of ninety-seven. At the time we were shot down, Gordon was married to Gladys V. Siegrist of Zurich. The couple would have two children, Robert and Joan. I was honored to know that Lt. Commander Kennington gave me credit for saving his life.

The second time I was shot down came toward the end of December 1943; we had received orders to return to Perth, Australia, for three months of rest. Before we left, we were training members of VP-22 on what rescue operations in the area looked like. We received word from Port Moresby that a B-25 had been shot down; a couple of P-40s were protecting the five crew members in the water, and they wanted to know if we could get a plane up there and conduct a rescue.

Even though our crew was due to leave the next day for Perth, we volunteered to pick up the B-25 crew. The group we were training had never been up in that area, so we told them to fly behind us and observe how we performed a rescue.

When we arrived at the location, we noticed that the plane's five-person crew had made it into the plane's lifeboat. While the seas were a little rough, they were not in any immediate danger, so we began circling the area, trying to get a read on the white-caps and figuring out the best way to land between the swells. As we started to drop in elevation, one of the P-40s that had been protecting the men somehow mistook us for a Japanese plane coming in to strafe the guys in the water.

The P-40 fired at us and shot us down. Now there were two crews in the water. The B-25 crew had a lifeboat, and our crew did not, so the PBY that was with us landed and picked us up. After we got aboard, I went to the cockpit and took control of the wheel. We made our way to the five men from the B-25, picked up the crew, and then headed back.

Sadly, unlike the first time we were shot down, when we suffered no casualties, this time one of our crewmen, our bow gunner, was fatally wounded. Losing a man in combat is bad enough, but losing a man to friendly fire is horrible.

A few days later, Army General Douglas MacArthur, who was the supreme commander of the Southwest Pacific area, and who would later go on to become one of only five Army officers to reach the rank of five-star general (the others being John J. Pershing, George C. Marshall, Dwight D. Eisenhower, Henry H. Arnold, and Omar Bradley), visited us in the hospital and expressed his condolences regarding the man we had lost.

I was always impressed by General MacArthur's visit to the hospital; he cared about the men in his command, and he made sure that each man under his leadership knew it.

10

THE AUSTRALIAN
COASTWATCHERS

IN LATE NOVEMBER, WE had just returned from an all-night flight when the skipper came up to me and one of our other crew members and said, "Come up to the wardroom for breakfast; you guys are ensigns." And that was it—I had received my commission. I was now an officer in the US Navy. I was proud to have received my commission; however, to be completely honest, I did not have much time to give too much thought to what that meant precisely or what it all entailed. We were simply too busy.

During this time, we had been dropping off many of the Australian Coastwatchers, who were Allied military intelligence operatives stationed on remote Pacific islands during the war. The mission of the Coastwatchers was to observe enemy movements and rescue stranded Allied personnel. They played a significant role in the Pacific Ocean theatre and southwest Pacific theatre, particularly as an early warning network during the Guadalcanal campaign.

In the middle of December, General Kinney called us together and told us that there were over two hundred Coastwatchers caught behind enemy lines. We had transported many of these guys to their drop-off locations at the start of their mission. They would backpack their way into the mountains, carrying all their equipment, including their radio gear, to relay information back to our forces on the Japanese troops' and fleet movement. They were like our Navy SEALs and Green Berets of today's military. The information they provided was extremely valuable.

The Japanese had brought an entire division of men (fifteen thousand in total) into the area and were sending two thousand men at a time to locate the Coastwatchers. Everyone knew it was going to be a tough mission, not only because we would be working behind enemy lines but also because the area where the Australian Coastwatchers were stranded was right in the middle of headhunter territory.

Most of the tribes in the area were hostile to outsiders. Even more, the tribesmen would eat any outsiders they caught; that's right—they were cannibals, or at least that was what we were told.

There was one tribe, however, that was friendly toward the Australians. It seemed the Australians had developed a relationship with this group over the years, and the friendship proved to be unbelievably valuable during the war. The Australians had taken good care of them, so they were on noneating terms.

We knew that to remain undetected by the Japanese, we would have to fly low to the ground and follow the Sepik River path; we simply could not fly from point A straight to point B. If we had been able to fly using a straight shot, it would have been about 150 miles each way, but we had to travel just off the river's water and follow each twist and turn, which made the trip approximately 470 miles long. We only had about fifteen to twenty feet of clearance from the dense jungle on each of our wingtips.

We would work our way upriver, and when we arrived at the village, the tribesmen would come out to the plane and pull us to shore. They would help us load the aircraft with fifteen to seventeen Coastwatchers and their gear, and then they would push us back into the river.

We would go full blast down the river, and once we reached a speed between sixty and seventy knots, we'd make a big turn and then accelerate to eighty-five knots and start climbing into the clouds to avoid the Japanese Zeros. Our PBYs were stripped of weapons and other weight, so we could climb quickly into the clouds to evade Japanese Zeros if necessary (and to carry more people).

Each mission was fairly intense as every crew member believed that if we got shot down, or if we crashed a plane, we were destined to become crocodile food, prisoners of the Japanese, or end up on a spit, slow cooking as the feature dish at one of the tribes' barbecues. When they said it was cannibal country, they meant it—as we soon found out for ourselves during one of our missions.

I'm not sure I would have believed the whole cannibal story had it not been for one of the encounters we had with one of the "friendly" tribes. We had just landed and were loading some of the Coastwatchers and their gear when the chief of the tribe approached us and asked us to stay for a big barbecue the next day. He was going to send a few of his men to a neighboring tribe to get a young twelve- to fourteen-year-old girl and bring her back for a barbecue. I remember making the excuse that we would have loved to stay but were expected back; I said that when we completed our mission, we would come back and have a barbecue with them. We did not want to say no since we figured if we insulted them, they would not have been too happy with us and might have barbecued us that night.

In three days, five crews from VP-11 rescued all 219 Coastwatchers, who would have otherwise been captured or killed by the Japanese. It was one of the most significant rescues in World

War II, but no one knew about it because everything about the Coastwatchers was top secret in those days. The best part about the mission—we did not lose a single man.

Seventy-five years later, I would learn that the Australian Air Force did not, and still does not, allow their people to fly over that area of New Guinea or specific regions of the Sepik River because if they have any trouble and have to bail out, they're barbecue the next day.

For my contributions to the rescue, I was awarded the Distinguished Flying Cross for Valor, and to this day, I consider my participation in the event to be one of the most significant accomplishments of my career.

On June 18, 1944, my mother received a letter from Lt. General George C. Kenney, commanding officer of headquarters of the Fifth Air Force. The letter read as follows:

Dear Mrs. Conter:

Recently your son, Ensign Louis A. Conter, was decorated with the Distinguished Flying Cross. It was an award made in recognition of courageous service to his combat organization, his fellow American airman, his country, his home and to you.

He was cited for extraordinary achievement while participating in aerial flights in the Southwest Pacific area from September 13th to December 30th, 1943.

Your son took part in a sustained operational flight missions during which hostile contact was probable and expected. These flights aided considerably in the recent successes in this theater.

Almost every hour of every day your son, and the sons of other American mothers, are doing just such things as that here in the Southwest Pacific.

There is a very real and very tangible contribution to victory and peace.

I would like to tell you how genuinely proud I am to have such men as your son in my command, and how gratified I am to know the young Americans with such courage and resources are fighting our country's battle against the aggressor nations.

You, Mrs. Conter, have every reason to share that pride and gratification.

Very sincerely,

George C. Kenney,

Lieutenant General, Commanding

I was especially proud of my time as a naval aviator in the Southwest Pacific area and more specifically my contributions to helping rescue many of the 219 Australian Coastwatchers from New Guinea.

Many years later, I received one of the most prestigious honors of my life when I was inducted into the Maritime Patrol and Reconnaissance Force Hall of Honor at the Heritage Dinner on April 26, 2017. The group recognizes and honors men and women who have helped shape the heritage of the maritime patrol and reconnaissance and/or displayed acts of heroism in and out of combat. Much like my being awarded the Distinguished Flying Cross for Valor, I consider my recognition for this award to be reflective of not just my actions but also the actions of each man who participated in this heroic effort.

On December 30, 1943, VP-11 was transferred to Palm Island, Australia, and was taken off combat operations for a while and began conducting routine administrative and passenger flights to Port Moresby, Samari, and Brisbane.

By the end of 1943, I had been promoted to the rank of

lieutenant junior grade (Lt. JG) and was given orders to report to Whidbey Island and Oak Harbor, Washington, where I was going to be trained as a patrol plane commander (PPC) with the idea of going back into a PBY with a duty station in the Philippines.

Shortly after the New Year, I was due for my annual physical, during which doctors discovered I had a heart murmur. I was put in the Navy hospital in Brisbane and then transferred by ship to San Diego, where I would undergo several weeks of testing at another naval hospital.

In his book *Black Cats and Dumbos* (1988), Mel Croker states:

> The story of the PBY Catalina Patrol Member is not just a tale of an ugly-duckling seaplane scheduled for the scrapheap that was pressed into emergency service when the world became embroiled in war; neither is it just a biography of a group of brave, dedicated men whose trust in that aircraft developed into an almost fanatical fair; rather, it is the incredible, almost unbelievable, true accounting of a naval aircraft, and the men who flew it.

I consider myself lucky to have been one of the men who served aboard a PBY. After logging over two thousand hours of flight time, having been shot down not once but twice, and flying that plane in the worst weather and environmental conditions imaginable, I can say without reservations that the PBY was a great plane.

11

Sent to the States

I WAS PLACED ON a Jeep carrier in Brisbane, Australia, and sixteen days later, I arrived in San Diego, California, where I was sent to the naval hospital in La Jolla. When I arrived at the hospital, I was not sure why I needed to be there. I understood the heart murmur issue, but there were guys hospitalized who needed to be hospitalized; there were guys with serious wounds, guys who had shrapnel throughout their bodies, and guys who had lost limbs.

After a few rounds of testing, my doctors came to me and said they still did not know what they were going to do with me. There was talk of my being permanently grounded, and there was talk of my being discharged from the Navy. Eventually, they determined my condition was not life-threatening, so I was discharged from the hospital and moved to a facility known as US Naval Hospital, Unit 6. It was there where I underwent more tests with a heart specialist.

Unit 6 was operated as an annex to the main Naval Hospital San Diego, located in Balboa Park in the city center. The facility was essentially a convalescent home for injured officers during World War II.

The US Naval Hospital, Unit 6, began operating in February

1943 and housed up to sixty ambulatory naval officers. The facility was designed to assist in the recovery of patients released from Naval Hospital San Diego until they retired or returned to duty (US Navy, 2020). The grounds and facilities were terrific. You could do a variety of activities or just walk the grounds. There were orchards that grew a variety of fruit such as oranges, tangerines, pears, peaches, and even avocados, all available for the picking.

The area where it is located, Rancho Santa Fe, is just a few miles from the beach, so from time to time, we would leave the grounds and head to the ocean. A few of us liked to spend our free time just playing around a bit, swimming, or hanging out.

One day, a few of us went to Del Mar Beach. We saw three girls coming our way, and when we met up, we ended up talking to them for a while. They asked us what we did and where we were from. We shared that we were all in the military, that we had been hurt in the war, and that we were being treated for various injuries at the Navy hospital. I took a liking to one of the gals, Katie Loftus. She was cute, smart, very friendly, had a good sense of humor, and, oh, did I say she was cute? Katie and her friends were celebrating their graduation from the University of Southern California, and they had rented a place on the beach for a week.

Things went so well with all of us that we planned to meet later that night for dinner, but only two of us decided to go. I went, of course, along with a friend of mine, Leonard Schultz, who was a lieutenant in the Marine Corps.

We went back to Rancho Santa Fe, showered, and changed into our dress uniforms to meet with the girls. One thing about being in the military: when you dress, you automatically dress to impress. Your shoes are shined, your brass is polished, your gig line is straight, and if you had been in combat, like just about everyone in World War II, you had lots of ribbons and probably a few medals displayed on your chest. That evening, when we saw the girls—or, rather, when they saw us—I think the uniforms genuinely impressed them. They did not hurt; that's for sure.

It was a great evening. Katie and I talked most of the night, and we had a wonderful time getting to know one another. I found out she was a member of the Kappa Alpha Theta sorority when she was a student at the University of Southern California, she was a member of the Juniors of the League for Crippled Children, and she served as a nurse's aide. She seemed like a real down-to-earth girl. She found out a little about my upbringing and my Navy career. By the end of the night, we had become well acquainted, and one thing was sure: I wanted to see more of her, and I did.

We saw each other a few more times, always in the presence of her friends and mine, and then one day she said she wanted me to meet her parents. So we drove up to her parents' house in Beverly Hills, which was about one hundred miles north of San Diego.

I found her parents, Ed and Henrietta Loftus, to be good people. Ed was in the construction and real estate business and was very, very successful. Their house was beautiful, and even though you could tell they had money, you would never know it by the way Ed acted; he was just a regular guy. He was that way his entire life.

On Sunday, we attended church at the Church of the Good Shepherd on Roxbury Drive in Beverly Hills. The church was the oldest in Beverly Hills and was beautiful. I think the fact that I was Catholic went a long way to win over Katie's parents. I had taken Holy Communion during our visit, and later that evening, on our way back to Rancho Santa Fe, Katie shared with me how impressed her parents were that I did that. *Heck,* I remember thinking, *I'm a Catholic, and taking Holy Communion is what Catholics do.*

I enjoyed spending time with Katie, and we started spending more and more of it together. She was a great gal, and we were having a lot of fun.

Toward the middle of May, my doctor said, "Lou, you have an innocent heart murmur." I asked, "What in the world is an innocent heart murmur?" My doctor smiled and said, "It's the kind that's innocent, so I'm clearing you to return to flying." And, just like that, I was back to being a Navy aviator again.

I remember thinking to myself, *Boy, this is excellent news*, but I also remember thinking I would have to break the news to Katie. I would be returning to flying and leaving for my next duty, the Naval Air Station on Whidbey Island just north of Oak Harbor, Washington; I was going to be a long way from Beverly Hills, California.

When I told Katie that I was healthy and the murmur was nothing to worry about, she was pretty happy. When I told her that the Navy had declared me fit for duty and I would be leaving soon for my next duty station in the state of Washington, I could see her disappointment, but after a moment, she smiled and said, "That's great. I love you, so I think we should just get married, and I'll go with you. What do you think?"

Well, I thought it was a great idea, so, after knowing each other for about three months, we decided to get married. I was twenty-three, and she was twenty-two, and just like that, we were both headed for a new adventure.

On May 27, 1944, we announced our engagement at a magnificent luncheon that Ed and Henrietta put on for us at the Jonathan Club in Santa Monica, California. The club sits on Ocean Avenue and overlooks the beach, and back in the 1940s, just as it is today, the club was extremely exclusive.

The club's membership included a number of well-known leaders of industry, businessmen, politicians, movie moguls, and even a few military men, including Rear Admiral Isaac Campbell

Kidd, with whom I served aboard the USS *Arizona* and who perished on December 7, 1941.

Katie and I were married at high noon on June 10, 1944, in the Cathedral Chapel in Los Angeles. Katie was a beautiful bride. She wore a white satin gown trimmed with seed pearls and carried her prayer book and a bouquet of orchids. Leonard Schultz was my best man, and Lt. Horace Fritz, Ensign Lee Schmidt, and Katie's brother, Edward, were my ushers. It was a great wedding. We had about three hundred people attend, and then after, we went to Ed and Henrietta's home for our reception.

Later that evening, we jumped in Katie's Chevy Coupe and took off for Santa Barbara, where we spent our first night as husband and wife. The next night, we were in San Francisco, and the following day we pushed our way to Oak Harbor, Washington. We rented a house in Mount Vernon, and I reported for duty a few days later.

I had not been at my new duty station very long before we received word that the Navy was going to transfer three PBNs to go from Elizabeth, North Carolina, to Kodiak, Alaska, where the United States was going to turn the planes over to the Russians.

The planes the Russians were getting were a variation of the American Consolidated Aircraft Company PBY series. Interestingly, the Naval Aircraft Factory in Philadelphia took the original design and produced some major improvements and changed its military identifier from a Y to an N, so the new plane became the PBN-1 Nomad. The new aircraft had several differences from the basic PBY in that it had a revised hull; revised wingtip floats; a unique nose turret; a longer, pointed nose; a longer fuselage; and a taller tail (Pelley, 2020). Essentially, it flew the same, and since I had so much experience in the PBY, I was one of three aviators told to pick out a crew and fly back East to help with the transfer.

When we arrived in Washington, DC, they placed us on temporary additional duty with the Russian Air Force. When we went to get the PBNs, we found that they were already painted with Russian markings, including the big red stars.

The next morning, we took off from Washington on our way to our first stop, Fort Worth, Texas. Our progress was good until we reached Shreveport, where we had a couple of fighters from the Army Air Corp training station pull up beside us and message us that we were to identify ourselves and immediately land.

Because our planes had no wheels and Shreveport had no water, we couldn't land. Thus, we decided to do a flyover of the runway. As we approached the runway, the general of the base got on the radio and said, "Lower your wheels and prepare to land." One of the other pilots in our group replied, "You stupid son of a bitch, we're Navy pilots. We don't have any wheels." Then we passed over the runway at about one hundred feet off the ground. When we had cleared, we just pushed the throttle up, climbed to eight thousand feet, and continued to Fort Worth. We did not hear another word from the tower, nor did anyone follow us.

We reached Fort Worth, landed, gassed up, and then headed out to San Diego. As we approached San Diego, we hit a marine layer, an air mass that develops over the ocean in the presence of a temperature inversion. The inversion itself is usually initiated by the cooling effect of the water on the surface layer of an otherwise warm air mass. As it cools, the surface air becomes denser than the warmer air above it and thus becomes trapped below it. The result is fog.

When the weather was bad in San Diego, military planes were usually detoured to El Centro, where the fog was often less dense. Planes that needed water to land would be put down in the Salton Sea, a shallow, saline, endorheic lake located in the Imperial and Coachella Valleys.

As you approached San Diego from the east, there was a big, lit arrow that pointed to El Centro, which the Navy had constructed; if San Diego was closed, the arrow was lit, and you were supposed to detour. If the arrow was not lit, you were to continue to San Diego. The arrow was lit, but since none of us wanted to risk getting fogged in at El Centro, we decided to keep going to San Diego; besides we knew our girls were just a short drive away, and if we got lucky, we might get fogged in for a few days.

Sure enough, as we got closer to San Diego, the fog was pretty bad, but when we dropped down to land in Mission Bay, the fog broke at about one hundred feet. We had excellent visibility, and we were able to land safely and taxi to the docks.

One of the attending seamen informed us that they were closed and that we should have detoured to El Centro. We told him we had no idea how bad the weather was and that we had not seen the detour light on our approach. By the look on his face, I think he knew we were lying.

Katie was in Southern California visiting her parents, so I called her up, and she came down. We were fogged in for three days, and Katie and I had a pleasant stay at the Coronado Hotel.

When the weather cleared, Katie went back to her parents' house, and I, along with my crew and the other pilots and their crews, all left for Kodiak, Alaska.

All along the Pacific coast, the weather was terrible, so much so that we had to use instruments much of the way; then, about a half an hour from Kodiak, the sun came out, giving us the best weather we had since we had left San Diego.

After we landed, we checked in with the Russians, got acquainted with them, and talked back and forth for the rest of the day (we had a translator). The next day, we took them through taxiing the planes, taking off, and landing, and then on the third day, they went out to their aircraft and looked them over. Their commanding officer said, "Okay, let's go," and the others all got into their planes and took off. Later that afternoon, we hitched a ride to Anchorage and flew back to Oak Harbor.

About two or three months later, we got word that the Navy wanted to send eight or ten of us down to Jacksonville, Florida, to fly the F-7-F, the first twin-engine fighter used by the US Navy. There were very few of us qualified for night flying, but due to my PBY experience, I had a significant amount of time flying at night, so I was off to Jacksonville again. I put the fighter through the paces and made the standard rolls, banks, and loops, and then shortly after we had finished checking out the plane, we were given orders to go to the Philippines, where we would be based on a carrier.

A few nights before our group was to head out, some of us were having a few drinks at the officers' club when my old executive officer from VP-11, Steve Johnson, walked in. Commander Johnson was now Captain Johnson, and he had just been transferred to Jacksonville to serve as the Navy's assignment officer.

The Germans had surrendered in May 1945, so everyone was focusing their attention on the war in the Pacific. When Captain Johnson found out we were due to ship out to the Philippines, he said, "You guys are not going. You've had too much already." He knew we had been in the fight. Hell, he was with us all throughout our time with VP-11, and in his eyes, maybe he was thinking we had already contributed enough to the war in terms of being in combat.

Regardless of what his thoughts were, within three days, all of us had other assignments. My assignment was to become the commanding officer of TDD unit #1. In other words, I was put in charge of the Navy's first drone unit. TDD stood for Target Drone Denny, which was a type of target drone that was very effective for antiaircraft training.

As the forerunners of modern target drones and RPVs (aerial

SENT TO THE STATES   85

vehicles that are remotely piloted), these midget radio-controlled aircraft gave the antiaircraft gunnery crews just what they needed for target practice. First of all, these were targets that looked like aircraft, sounded like aircraft, and flew like full-size aircraft. They could even simulate attack maneuvers (Denny & Righter, 2012).

I was shipped out to Lake City, Florida, for a few months and received training on various planes and drones. It was not too long before the Navy discovered that it was not a good idea to practice with drones at the same location where you were training young pilots. So, due to safety issues, TDD-1 was transferred to Norman, Oklahoma.

When I first heard that we were being transferred to Oklahoma, I remember thinking to myself, *Why the hell would they have a naval training base in Oklahoma?* There was not any water there. But they did, and the Naval Air Station in Norman had been a training base since the early part of the war.

I was not sure what to think of the whole drone program, but if I had any misgivings, they became moot in August of 1945, when the United States detonated two nuclear weapons over the Japanese cities of Hiroshima (August 6, 1945) and Nagasaki (August 9, 1945).

The atomic bombing of Japan was necessary. After Germany's surrender, the Japanese had planned an all-out defense of the island. In all, there were 2.3 million Japanese Army troops prepared to defend the home islands, backed by a civilian militia of twenty-eight million men and women. Casualty predictions varied widely but were extremely high. The vice chief of the Imperial Japanese Navy general staff, Vice Admiral Takijirō Ōnishi, predicted up to twenty million Japanese deaths (Giangreco, 2009). The Japanese were bound by the Code of Bushido, which is the refusal to surrender and the belief it was more honorable to die, even commit *hari-kari* (which is a ritual suicide by self-disembowelment on a sword), than to become a prisoner of war.

In addition to the staggering number of Japanese losses, the US government wartime casualty assessments provided a chilling reminder of the human cost of an invasion had President Harry Truman decided not to drop the atomic bombs on Hiroshima and Nagasaki. The lowest number of estimated fatalities would have cost America approximately 280,000 lives. Other assessments go as high as half a million or one million fatalities, with many more being wounded. As horrendous as these predictions were, they may well be underestimates. Postwar access to captured Japanese documents and senior Japanese military leaders indicate Japan had greater military forces available to defend the homeland than US officials predicted (Klinger, 2016).

The day after Nagasaki was bombed (August 10, 1945), Emperor Michinomiya Hirohito knew the war was over and on August 15, 1945 (August 14, 1945, in the United States due to time zone differences), announced that his country will accept unconditional surrender and called for a ceasefire that formally ended World War II. On September 2, 1945, the formal signing of the Japanese Instrument of Surrender took place onboard the battleship USS *Missouri* in Tokyo Bay; and just like that, the war was over.

By mid-September, the Navy began to downsize, and since there was no longer a need for drones or drone training, they disbanded the squadron, and I was given orders to report to Tustin, California.

I was extremely excited to be going to California; not only was I going to be reunited with Katie, but I was going to meet my son, Edward Michael Conter, who was born on July 16, 1945.

Due to my military responsibilities, I was unable to take leave when Michael was born, so I did not get to hold my child until he was two and a half months old, and I must say, while

I had been around other babies and held those children in my arms, holding Michael was one of the greatest experiences of my life. I thought to myself, *Wow, this child is mine.* I was completely overwhelmed and so very grateful to be a dad. Katie and I had a son. It was amazing.

12

THE CALM BEFORE THE STORM

AT THE END OF World War II, the US government owned vast quantities of war materials no longer needed for military purposes. Estimates of the value of the probable surpluses ranged from a low of $25 billion to a high of $150 billion. The surpluses included almost every conceivable article and commodity—some were of little utility in a peaceful world, others in great demand by the civilian populations of the United States and other countries (CQ Researcher, 1943).

When I received my orders to report to Tustin, California, I was assigned to the blimp hangars—not to fly blimps but to sell Navy surplus items to the public. If you have never seen or heard of the Tustin blimp hangars (there were two of them built), they are very unusual structures. Designed and built on a hyper-accelerated schedule during the war, in 1942, and with a nearly all-wood design, the hangars were made seventeen stories high, over one thousand feet long, and three hundred feet wide; they are still to this day one of the largest wooden structures ever built (City of Tustin California, 2020).

Imagine those two structures filled with everything you can

think of, from the massive amounts of equipment and unused military uniforms to office supplies to vehicles; you name it, we had it, and for three months, my job was to sell these items. I must be honest, selling Navy surplus equipment was a god-awful job; it sure as hell was not like flying.

One benefit of being assigned this duty was that one of the guys with me in Tustin was a golfer. One day, he said, "Lou, why don't you come golfing with me?" When I told him I had never golfed, he said, "Don't worry about it. You're an athlete. I'll teach you," and he did. I was hooked after my first round, and golf became one of the great joys in my life.

With the end of the war, Katie and her parents wanted me out of the Navy. Ed, being the tremendous businessman he was, said that he thought it would be a good idea for me to learn as much as I could about being a businessman. He had a ton of construction and real estate businesses, so when I became educated and trained on how to be a good businessman, I could make a great life for our growing family.

I had been in the Navy for only six years anyway, so I thought, *What the hell? Why not?,* and I put in for a discharge.

At first, the Navy said no. I had too much experience, and they were not ready to just let guys walk away. A few weeks later, however, they came up with a point system that would determine if someone could get a discharge or not. If you had three thousand points, you could get out. I had forty-eight thousand points.

The Navy came back and said that they would allow me to leave the regular Navy as long as I signed up for the Reserves. They were willing to make me a lieutenant in the Reserves, and all I would have to do was report for duty one weekend a month at Los Alamitos and provide briefings and training to the pilots. We had about four or five squadrons running out of Los Alamitos at the time, so the workload was light.

It all sounded good to me, so I said okay, received my honorable discharge, and was sworn into the Reserves as a lieutenant in the Navy.

Katie, Michael, and I moved into a home in Whittier. As I have said previously, Ed Loftus was a very generous man. Not only did he buy us our home in Whittier, but he named me the vice president of one of his construction companies (he had several). If that was not enough, he gave me one-third ownership in that business, encouraged me to go to college, and agreed to pay for it. He was amazing.

In the spring of 1946, I applied to and was accepted at the University of Southern California, where I began pursuing my degree in business administration.

I had a busy schedule. I went to school every Monday, Wednesday, and Friday from 8:00 a.m. until 12:00 p.m. and then went to the office, where I worked from 1:00 p.m. until 5:00 p.m. I was also taking classes for my real estate license and real estate broker's license, both of which I received in 1946 and still maintain to this day.

The next few years flew by fairly quickly. It was a very busy time in our lives. The first track of houses we built was in Whittier. We put up 120 homes, and they sold quickly. You have to keep in mind that after the war, the housing industry in Southern California exploded. Jobs were plentiful, the climate was perfect almost year round, and the newly formed Federal Housing Administration helped returning veterans finance homes by guaranteeing loans with more extended repayment periods, offsetting what had been a shortage of affordable housing.

With the first track of houses selling out so quickly, we decided to buy a big piece of property along the Santa Ana Freeway, just east of Norwalk. This time, we built 509 houses. The housing market was booming, and we were on the ground floor.

Even though we were working hard, one thing I learned from

Ed was to make sure I took time off from time to time. As I shared earlier, I had started to golf when I was selling surplus, and soon, I had started playing just about every weekend.

I started golfing more and more with Ed, who was a darn good golfer and a member of the Wilshire Country Club. One of his good friends was Jack Temple, Shirley Temple's father. Jack was a member of the Bel-Air Country Club, so I played golf just about every weekend. On Saturday, we would golf at the Wilshire Country Club, and then on Sunday, we would golf at the Bel-Air Country Club. John Agar, who was Shirley's husband, usually completed our foursome.

As everyone knows, Shirley was an American sweetheart and was Hollywood's number-one box office draw as a child actress in the late 1930s, but in the mid-'40s, she had stepped away from making films and was finishing up her schooling at the Westlake School for Girls in Los Angeles. Shirley met John in 1943 through his sister, who was also a student at the school.

John was in the military during World War II, served in the Navy Air Corps, and spent much of his military career as a physical training instructor at March Field in Riverside, California. When John and Shirley married, she was seventeen, and he was twenty-four.

One day, during a round of golf, John told me he was working toward being an actor. He had met Shirley at a party hosted by David O. Selznick a few years earlier and had even been signed to a contract, but although he had been taking acting lessons for almost two years, he still had not appeared in a movie. He asked me what I thought of the idea of his being an actor. I told him to look around at the people with big money, the members of the country clubs. I told him, "You should go to school, get your college degree, and go into personal investment financing." Well, I don't think that was the answer he was hoping to hear. He was dead set on becoming an actor.

John stuck with things, and it ended up paying off for him. In 1948, he made his film debut as Shirley's love interest in *Fort Apache*, which starred Shirley, John Wayne, and Henry Fonda and was directed by John Ford.

I had the chance to spend a lot of time with John, and I always felt he and Shirley never belonged together. I had gotten to know her pretty well, and, in fact, we became good friends. I liked her, but I always saw John as a social climber and felt he was using Shirley to further his acting career.

As it turned out, I was probably right because, in 1950, Shirley and John got divorced. It was a pretty bad divorce, and John took the wrath of the media. Shirley was still a popular movie star, and John . . . well, he fell on hard times, so much so that he ultimately ended up only being able to land roles in B-movies. Things worked out for Shirley, however, as she met a great guy named Charles Alden Black, a Navy man, whom I will talk about a bit later in this chapter.

On September 23, 1946, Katie gave birth to our second son, Anthony (Tony). Unlike the birth of Michael, I was there for Tony's birth.

Just as I was with Michael, I was completely overwhelmed and incredibly grateful to be a dad. The excitement was the same, and holding Tony in my arms created the same feelings I had experienced with our first son.

For most of 1947 and part of 1948, I was living a regular life. Katie and I had two children, I was working full time, and I was doing my monthly reserve duty in Los Alamitos; I was enjoying being a husband and father.

Ed bought some property in San Diego, enough for five hundred lots and homes, and was well on his way to becoming one of Southern California's biggest construction guys. Ed had a hand in several businesses, including the Young and Loftus Construction Company, the Loftus Land Company, the Sunshine

Financial Corporation, and the Sunshine Water Company—four separate companies that all had to do with building up a home from the ground level. He was also a part of Financial Corporation, a home financing company that financed the homes being built. Ed was making and financing homes for veterans and anyone else who bought one, until they could get FHA or VA loans, and had every aspect of the build-out covered, from bare lots to completion of the financing.

He was a brilliant businessman. As for those five hundred homes? We sold them in twenty-one days. I was somewhat confident that once my time in the Navy was complete, I would be spending the rest of my life working in construction and real estate. I was wrong.

Soon after World War II ended, the Russians, who had been our allies in the battle against the Axis powers (Germany, Italy, and Japan), under their dictator, Joseph Stalin, acted to solidify their wartime conquests and advance the cause of worldwide Marxist Leninism, an ideology that subverted the very ideals most Americans then held sacred (Marolda, 2020). These Russian actions created a period of geopolitical tension between the United States and the Soviet Union, an era in our history that became known as the Cold War.

Our military was once again preparing for war; they knew it, but few civilians did, nor did they want to know. We were just a few short years past the end of World War II, and life for most people was just returning to some type of normal. For those in the military, however, the memories of Pearl Harbor and being caught by a surprise attack were still fresh; being unprepared again for a possible attack was unthinkable, so the training of our military continued, and one of the most significant intelligence reorganizations of the immediate postwar period occurred in September 1945, when President Harry S. Truman abolished the Office of Strategic Services (Public Affairs, Central

Intelligence Agency, 2008). This event preceded the January 1946 creation of the Central Intelligence Group (later the Central Intelligence Agency). The establishment of the Department of Defense in 1947 then influenced the subsequent development of the nation's intelligence structure (Williamsom, Jones, Myers, Marshall, & Williamsom, 2020).

In 1948, the Navy placed me on active duty, and I was sent to intelligence school in Washington, DC, for five and a half months. The course of study was very intense and included instruction in cryptology and communications security. The training was fascinating to me, and I enjoyed being in the intelligence field a great deal. I had my suspicions that there was another world conflict looming in the future, but I just was not sure when or where that situation would be happening.

When I completed my training, I returned to California, and it was back to the business of building and selling homes. On March 1, 1949, Katie and I had another boy, and even though John was our third child, I was still completely overwhelmed and so incredibly grateful to be a dad. I took tremendous joy in being a father, and I was grateful for all my blessings.

Later that year, the Navy again sent me to school; this time, I went to San Diego, where I took classes in photographic, air, and radar intelligence, and I also attended ABC school, which is atomic, biological, and chemical warfare training.

Even though I was not very far from home, I would say this was probably about the time when my still being in the military started to create a little bit of a rift in the family. Although I was technically a reservist, the Navy was sending me to more and more trainings. I think another factor that probably was irritating to some family members (mostly my mother-in-law, Henrietta) was that I had to drop out of USC. I had completed all but about fifteen units, and I just couldn't find the time to finish up that last semester.

While I think Katie was okay with things, Henrietta started to drop hints that she was not too happy about me still being in the Navy and being away from home. I understood her point, but I did not have much choice; when the Navy ordered me to do something, I had to do what I was ordered to do.

On June 25, 1950, I was working at the Loftus Land and Construction office in Whittier when Katie came in with a telegram that had been delivered to the house from the Department of the Navy. The telegram stated that I was to report immediately for active duty in San Diego. When I called the Department of the Navy and asked what was going on, they said, "We're at war with North Korea," and just like that, I was back on active duty.

Mary, Esther, and Lou Conter

High school yearbook picture

Early Navy days

Flight school, 1942

Getting into my PBY Catalina Blackcat

Commissioned Naval Aviator. US Navy Photograph

Left to right—Esther Conter (sister), Lou, Lottie Conter (mother),
Nicholas Conter (father) and Mary (sister)

Receiving a commendation. US Navy Photograph

Lieutenant Lou Conter. US Navy Photograph

Lou, late 1940s

Lou at SERE Training

Johnny Mathis, Corey Pavin, Lou Conter, and our fourth teammate:
winners of the Bob Hope Chrysler Classic

Lou, Val, and Louann Conter

Master Chief Jim Taylor, retired, right, Pearl Harbor Survivor Liaison at Navy Region Hawaii, greets Lou before the start of the 72nd anniversary commemoration of the Dec. 7, 1941 attack on Pearl Harbor. Seated with Lou is United States Park Ranger Amanda Carona Thompson. US Navy photo by Mass Communication Specialist 2nd Class Nardel Gervacio

Lou at the 76th Anniversary of the attack on Pearl Harbor.
US Navy photo by Petty Officer 2nd Class Katarzyna Kobiljak—Navy Public Affairs
Support Element Detachment Hawaii

Lou and Ed Bonner, friend and former Placer County sheriff.
US Navy photo by Cpl. Wesley Timm—U.S. Marine Corps Forces, Pacific

Lou and his Marine escort at the 78th Anniversary Ceremony of the attack on Pearl Harbor. Photograph by Annette C. Hull

Lou Conter, USS *Arizona* survivor, gives personal remarks about fellow survivor Lauren Bruner during his sunset internment ceremony as part of the 78th anniversary Pearl Harbor Remembrance Commemoration. The honor of internment aboard the USS *Arizona* is reserved only for surviving crew members of the Dec. 7, 1941 attacks. Bruner is the 44th and final survivor to join his shipmates within the memorial. US Navy photo by Mass Communications Specialist 1st Class Holly L. Herline

USS *Arizona* survivor Lou Conter salutes during fellow survivor Lauren Bruner's sunset internment ceremony. US Navy photo by Mass Communication Specialist 2nd Class Cole C. Pielop

Jack Kennedy, Lou, and Linda Kennedy

Mary Andrew Johanson and Lou

Four Generations of Conters, from left to right: Jessie Burton, Lou Conter, Joey Burton, Reid Austin (with glasses), Nathan Burton, Jacob Burton, Nicole Austin holding Holden Austin, Jesse Austin holding Finn Austin, Louann Conter (sitting)

Three of Lou's children at Lou's 99th birthday party: James, Louann, Lou, and Jeff

Lou at his 99th birthday party

13

THE KOREAN WAR

I GOT IN MY car and drove to San Diego, and by 5:00 p.m., I was on active duty again.

I would venture to guess there may be some people who do not know that the United States was involved in a war in Korea, so let me start this chapter by giving a very brief and straight-forward overview of how and why the United States became involved in the Korean War.

At the beginning of the twentieth century, Korea was a part of the Japanese empire. After World War II, the United States and the Soviet Union were left to decide what should be done with their enemy's imperial possessions, which included Korea. The Korean peninsula was divided in half along the thirty-eighth parallel; the Russians occupied the area north of the line, and the United States occupied the area to its south. On June 25, 1950, some seventy-five thousand soldiers from the North Korean People's Army poured across the thirty-eighth parallel, the boundary between the Soviet-backed Democratic People's Republic of Korea to the north and the pro-Western Republic of Korea to the south. This invasion was the first military action of the Cold War. By July, American troops had entered the war on South Korea's behalf (History, 2020). So, in short, the Korean

War was basically a confrontation between the forces of democracy and those of communism.

Katie had some misgivings about my returning to active duty, as did her mother, who told me to "tell the Navy you can't do it." She wanted me out of the military. Ed, on the other hand, said, "Lou, the United States is our country, so if the Navy needs you, you go. Don't worry about things here; I'll take care of everything." This was an incredibly selfless gesture on his part. He was getting ready to retire, and I know that he was grooming me to take over his companies.

He and Henrietta had bought a house on Catalina Island back in 1926, and the family liked to spend the summers on the island. When I received the telegram from the Navy, the kids were there with Ed and Henrietta. It was tough to leave my family, but it was my duty, so in July of 1950, I reported to El Centro, California, for gunnery training.

Shortly after I arrived, I came down with a horrible cold and upper respiratory infection. When I went to the hospital, they gave me a shot of some new wonder drug called penicillin. It was not too long before I started feeling better, so I went back to my normal activities.

We had received a day off, so I decided to sneak in a round of golf. After about eight holes, I could not walk. The next thing I knew, they were bringing a cart to take me back to the clubhouse. They flew me from El Centro back to San Diego, where I spent ten days in the hospital. It seems I was one of the 0.03 percent of the population who has a severe penicillin allergy.

After I recovered, I was put on limited duty; I was given a week off and then shipped out to Pensacola, Florida, to requalify for carrier training. While I was in Pensacola, I spent a lot of time training in the AD Skyraider aircraft, a carrier-based, single-seat, long-range, high-performance dive/torpedo bomber.

The Skyraider was produced too late to take part in World

War II but became the backbone of US Navy aircraft carrier and US Marine Corps strike aircraft sorties in the Korean War (1950–1953), with the first ADs going into action from Valley Forge with VA-55 on July 3, 1950 (Mersky, 1983).

I completed my retraining in May 1951 and was assigned to the USS *Bon Homme Richard*, under the command of Captain Cecil B. Gill. In addition to the captain, each ship had an intelligence officer. Each air group (attached to an aircraft carrier) had a commanding officer, and like the ship, each one had an intelligence officer. I was the intelligence officer of Air Group 102. Our commanding officer was Commander H. N. Funk. Each squadron also had its own intelligence officer. Carrier Air Group 102 was assigned a complement of four squadrons, so we had five intelligence officers assigned to them. We had almost 150 pilots and over eighty aircraft.

We departed San Diego harbor for Hawaiian waters on May 7, 1951, and arrived in Pearl Harbor several days later. We were going to undergo a few weeks of training before continuing on to Korea, and since this was my first trip back to Hawaii since I had left the island in early 1942, I must say I had mixed emotions about being there.

I'm not sure how it came about, but I found myself, with four or five other guys, on the admiral's barge heading to the USS *Arizona*. The memorial had not been built yet, but in 1950, Admiral Arthur W. Radford, commander of the Pacific Fleet, had a platform installed over the USS *Arizona*'s sunken remains. He attached a flag pole to the mainmast and began a tradition of hoisting and lowering the flag. That same year, a temporary memorial was built above the remaining portion of the deckhouse. Radford requested funds for a national memorial in 1951 and 1952 but was denied because of budget constraints due to the war.

As we neared the USS *Arizona*, I was flooded with what seemed like hundreds of thoughts and memories. To be honest, it was too much to take. By the time we arrived at the platform, I had decided I was not going to disembark the barge; I just could not do it, so it was determined that we would not leave the barge and stand upon the platform. Instead, we would circle the USS *Arizona* and render a salute. I had to be a military man about it. It was awfully hard, but you have to do what is expected of you, and you always have to be as strong as possible.

Returning to the USS *Arizona* was an emotional experience for me; to this day, it is still hard to describe what I felt returning for the first time to the location of so much anguish and sorrow. My heart was heavy. As we pulled away from the USS *Arizona*, I said a prayer for all my shipmates whom we lost that day. It was such a tragedy—so many lost lives, so much sadness.

After spending some time reflecting on my trip to the USS *Arizona*, I received a call from an old friend that instantly warmed my heart. Shirley Temple was in Hawaii. She found out I was there as well, and she wanted to do lunch so I could meet her new husband, Charles Black. As mentioned earlier, Black, like me, was a Navy man, and at the outbreak of the Korean War, he had been called back to duty. I can't remember why they were in Hawaii; it might have been that Black was on leave.

I sure liked Charles. He was a good man, and he and Shirley ended up having a great life together. In 1952, Shirley gave birth to a son. After the war ended and Charles was discharged from the Navy, he would later manage KABC television in Los Angeles, while Shirley ended up being a homemaker—a role she excelled at. A few years later, they had another child, a daughter, who went on to have some success as a member of a rock band known as the Melvins. By the mid-'50s, Charles had become the director of business operations for the Stanford Research Institute (Windleler, 1978).

We had a pleasant visit. Shirley and I stayed in touch for a while, but eventually we lost track of one another. She went on to sit on the boards of several large corporations and organizations, including the Walt Disney Company, Del Monte Foods, and the National Wildlife Federation. She even represented the United States at a session of the UN General Assembly, where she worked at the US Mission under Ambassador Charles W. Yost. She was quite the gal.

On May 21, 1951, we left Pearl Harbor for Yokosuka, Japan, and were ordered to proceed to an action area and relieve the USS *Philippine Sea*. In doing so, we joined the USS *O'Brien* and the USS *Walke*, two Allen M. Sumner-class destroyers that were operating in the Korean Straits. By June, we had joined other units of Task Force 77 in action close to the thirty-eighth parallel.

Our mission was to conduct air operations from an operating area off the east coast of Korea, providing close air support for friendly troop operations, interdiction of enemy routes of movement and supplies, and armed reconnaissance of enemy installations and lines of communication. We also provided air cover for replenishment ships and other friendly naval surface forces when necessary, protected the fleet against air surface and subsurface attacks, provided error spotting to bombardment forces when directed, and performed photographic and visual reconnaissance as required. We coordinated air operations with the Fifth Air Force through JOC Korea. We also exchanged intelligence information with friendly naval forces engaged in surface interdiction operations on the east coast of Korea.

We began flying missions on May 31, 1950. From June 1, 1950, to July 28, 1950, I was involved in flying twenty-nine combat missions.

The *Bon Homme Richard* had a reliable crew, and we were very effective. When commenting on the performance of the USS *Bon Homme Richard*, the commanding officer of the USS *Princeton*, in a dispatch from July 13, said:

My sincerest, my sincere congratulations on the way the USS *Bon Homme Richard* has come in here cold and learned the business so quickly and well. Your air operations are at least as good as ours, and we have had eight months to practice. We know from experience from steaming in formation that the USS *Bon Homme Richard* will never put itself in a position to menace other ships in the force. To you and your Group, a sincere well done (History, 2020).

The commander of Task Force 77 said that it had been a personal pleasure to observe the outstanding performance of duty of the USS *Bon Homme Richard* and other detached squadrons during this tour in the operating area, and the combination of USS *Bon Homme Richard* and Carrier Air Group 102 is one that does credit to naval aviation.

In a very short period of time, while the Carrier Air Group 102 had inflicted significant damage to the enemy, we had also lost twelve aircraft, had 114 other aircraft damaged in battle, and lost seven pilots.

Shortly after the "Action Report for the period of May 31, 1951, through July 28, 1951" reached the chief of naval operations, a decision was made to ground all the intelligence officers. This, no doubt, was influenced by the fact that we had lost seven of our pilots. The Navy determined that we knew too much and that we were too valuable to risk being shot down and brought under the control of the North Koreans or Russians.

After I was grounded from carrier combat flights, most of my missions took place on the east coast of North Korea near the city of Masan, in the district of Changwon, a city in South Gyeongsang, South Korea.

Early in the Korean War, the Battle of Masan was an engagement between United Nations Command (UNC) and North

Korean forces, between August 5 and September 19, 1950, in the vicinity of Masan and the Naktong River in South Korea. It was part of the Battle of Pusan Perimeter and was one of several large engagements fought simultaneously. The battle ended in a victory for the UN after large numbers of US Army troops were able to repel the repeated attacks of two Korean People's Army (KPA) divisions (Wikipedia, 2020).

While I was still stationed aboard the USS *Bon Homme Richard*, my missions changed, and this is when I first met Herbie Brucker, an Army officer attached to the Office of Strategic Services, which was a wartime intelligence agency of the United States and a predecessor to the Central Intelligence Agency (CIA).

Some may recognize Herbie Brucker's name as he was one of the pioneers of the Army's elite Special Forces, also known as the Green Berets. I won't spend too much time on Herbie in this chapter. I will discuss him in more detail in an upcoming chapter, but for those wanting to sneak ahead, there are many articles regarding Herbie's contributions to the Green Berets and to the intelligence community in general, which can be easily found with a Google search.

I would fly from the USS *Bon Homme Richard* to Seoul, where I would pick up Herbie and his team, and then we would fly to wherever we needed to fly to and carry out our mission. I would fly the group back to Seoul, drop them off, and then fly back to the *Bon Homme Richard*. Herbie and his guys were a great group. They carried out a number of critical missions during their time in Korea, and I was proud to have served with them. Little did I know that I would cross paths again with Herbie Brucker at another duty station and that the two of us would become lifelong friends, but more on that later.

The USS *Bon Homme Richard* continued operations with Task Force 77 until November 20, 1951, when we departed for

San Diego, California, where we would arrive on December 19, 1951. When we pulled into the port, I was greeted by Katie and her parents. I had two weeks' leave coming, so we headed back to Whitter for a few days so that I could spend time with the kids over Christmas. Katie and I went to Arrowhead, which is in the San Bernardino Mountains of San Bernardino County, California. We had a great time; then I returned to San Diego for the week. The following Friday, I came back home again. As I was getting ready to leave for San Diego on Monday, Henrietta approached me and said, "I want you out of the Navy as soon as possible." I told her, "I don't think I can get out. There's still a war in Korea. I'm in a highly classified position, I'm a pilot, and I'm involved in intelligence."

Well, that did not sit well with Henrietta, so she sent a letter to the secretary of the Navy and demanded that he let me out.

A few weeks later, we both got a letter back from the secretary of the Navy stating that the Navy could not let me out because I was in such a critical position but that I could put in for discharge at the end of the war.

Not long after that letter arrived, I came home for the weekend, and Henrietta handed me divorce papers. I did not want a divorce, and I did not think Katie wanted one, but Henrietta did, so that was it. The marriage was over. I know this may sound strange to a few people, but I never really understood why Katie and I divorced. We never talked about it, ever.

We had a court hearing in Los Angeles. I went in my uniform, and Katie was there along with Henrietta and her attorney. The attorney spoke on behalf of the family. After about an hour, the judge, who was female, directed a question to the attorney: "I want to ask a question, Counselor." "Yes, Your Honor," the attorney replied. "Who is paying for this divorce?" Henrietta responded, "I am, Your Honor," to which the judge responded, "I thought so," and that was that.

The court required me to pay child support, to which I had no argument, but the judge had also known that the politics of wealth had come into play, probably more so than any other factor, so she set the amount at a meager number. Although I did not address the court, I believe the judge knew I did not want a divorce from Katie, and I think the judge knew Katie did not want to divorce me either; this was a Henrietta-driven divorce, plain and simple.

The entire proceeding took about an hour. Ed came to me and said if I did not contest the divorce, he would make sure the kids were taken care of and receive a proper education. True to his word, all the kids went on to get their college degrees and make a good life for themselves. The funny thing is even after Katie and I divorced, I stayed in contact with Ed; in fact, we talked almost once a month until he passed away in 1969.

I never looked at the divorce papers; I just signed them, gave Henrietta what she wanted, and decided to move on with my life.

We all know that being in the military is tough at times, and when I look back on my marriage with Katie, I think we did so many things right. The time we had together was great, and we had three magnificent children together.

I returned to San Diego and told my commanding officer I was getting a divorce. Then I reported back to the commander of the *Bon Homme Richard*, where I waited for the ship to return to sea. About two weeks had passed when I got a call from the head of the Office of Naval Intelligence in Los Angeles. "Lou," he said, "I understand you're getting a divorce."

"Yes, sir," I replied. "Well," he said, "I have a job for you, and I am going to have you transferred up here in a few days." Sure enough, I received orders to report to Naval Air Station Point Mugu, which had been an antiaircraft training center during World War II but had since become the Navy's major missile development and testing facility.

When I arrived at Point Mugu, I reported to the commander of the division at the time, Clyde Allen, and told him I was reporting for duty as the communications officer. My actual role was to investigate a suspected case of embezzlement. No one knew I was undercover, not even Commander Allen.

The location was basically a phone operators' terminal. There were twelve to fifteen girls working the phone lines for the private companies and contractors that were doing business on the base. There were a number of civilian contractors working at the naval air station; the communications department was in charge of paying the phone bill. The monthly bills for some of these groups could run upward of fifteen hundred dollars a month, and every month, someone from the company would come in and either write a check or pay cash for what they owed.

The Office of Naval Intelligence had determined that there was a shortage in the payments, and that was when they decided to send me in to figure out what was going on. I had an eavesdropping device installed in my office (which was basically just a phone hidden in my desk), and by listening to the phone conversations of all the girls in the office, I determined that the secretary who handled the money was the one responsible for the crime. If someone paid, say, fifteen hundred dollars in cash, which was common back then, she would take the cash, write them a receipt, and then write a duplicate receipt for eleven hundred dollars. She would then go into Commander Allen's office, have him sign the cooked books, and pocket four hundred dollars. Commander Allen had no idea what was going on.

I went to the bank, confirmed my suspicions, and then called down to the Office of Naval Intelligence and told them what was happening and how things were being done. By three that afternoon, I had orders to report to Washington, DC.

I went in and advised Commander Allen, and he chuckled and said, "Lou, I figured you wouldn't be here too long because you're too much of a fleet man to be in a job like this." I was out of there by five that evening.

The head of the Office of Naval Intelligence Division came up the following morning, and they arrested the secretary. It turned out that the girl, who was married with two children, had a boyfriend, a first-class petty officer, who was also married. The two were in the scam together.

Clyde Allen called me a few months later and said, "Lou, why didn't you tell me what you were there for?" I laughed and said, "I could not tell you that." Allen told me the girl had been sentenced to two years at the Tehachapi prison and that her husband had divorced her. The boyfriend had been court-martialed by the Navy. Not only was he charged with being a part of the theft, but back then the Navy could charge you with adultery, which they did. The boyfriend not only got kicked out of the Navy but also received some jail time.

I left Point Mugu and started a two-week leave. I went to Wenatchee, Washington, where I picked up my younger sister, Esther, and her husband, Chuck, who were learning how to be apple growers. We went on to my parents' house in Grand Junction, Colorado, where I spent a few days. Mom enjoyed seeing us, and it was a good visit.

I headed out to Kentucky, where I visited with my sister Mary, the nun. Mary enjoyed being a nun; she knew it was her calling. It was always good seeing her, and I am glad I had the chance to visit with her before heading into Washington, DC.

Once in DC, I received orders to report to Norfolk, Virginia, where I was assigned to be the intelligence officer for the commander of Fleet Air Wing Five. As the intelligence officer, I assisted in collecting, evaluating, and disseminating naval intelligence in support of surface, air, and antisubmarine warfare units and operational staff. I prepared and developed intelligence reports, and I began coordinating exercises with the OSS, Air Force AISS team, and elements of the CIA.

For those of you not familiar with these groups, as I mentioned earlier, the Office of Strategic Services (OSS) was a wartime intelligence agency of the United States during World War II and a predecessor to the CIA (Office of Strategic Services [OSS] Organization and Functions, 1945).

The OSS was formed as an agency of the Joint Chiefs of Staff (JCS) to coordinate espionage activities behind enemy lines for all branches of the US Armed Forces. Other OSS functions included the use of propaganda, subversion, and postwar planning (Clancey, 2020).

The Air Intelligence Service Squadron was an interesting group as they were "the first covert (military intelligence) collection agency in the United States Air Force history." Begun by Major Donald Nichols as an impromptu extension of his pre-Korean War espionage in 1950, it was first dubbed Special Activities Unit Number One. In April or May 1951, it officially became the 6004th Air Intelligence Service Squadron. The 6004th was an unorthodox unit that engaged in espionage and aircrew escape and evasion, as well as collecting information. It was the Far East Air Force's primary intelligence supplier for the war, generating as many as nine hundred reports per month (Haas, 2001).

In July 1950, Nichols set up an impromptu parachute training course so that espionage agents could be dropped behind the communist enemy's front lines. Shortly after that parachute behind North Korean lines, some of them would rescue the crew of a downed B-29 Superfortress. Forty-eight others would form the thirteen spy teams dropped behind enemy lines during this time; they spotted and reported rear area targets for the Air Force (Haas, 2001).

The CIA was created under the National Security Act of 1947, which President Truman signed on July 26, 1947, and officially came into existence on September 18 of that same year. President Truman appointed the Deputy Director of Central Intelligence Group (CIG) Roscoe H. Hillenkoetter as the first director of the CIA. One-third of the agency's personnel were OSS veterans (The Central Intelligence Agency, 2020).

As an intelligence officer, one of my responsibilities was to participate in reconnaissance missions. I enjoyed this specific aspect of my job, especially since it meant I was in a plane and flying, and I was right in the middle of the action. It just so happened that the admiral came in one day and said, "Conter, we've got some information that the Russians are cutting into the transatlantic telegraph cable north of Scotland, and we want you to report to Keflavik, Iceland, and find out what's going on."

I flew out to Iceland and jumped into a P2V, a long-range patrol aircraft, and we flew out over the north of Scotland. We spotted about fifteen or so boats of the Russian "fishing" fleet.

The P2V had a fairly large weapons bay, and we carried three pairs of 12.7mm machine-guns, so I told the gunners that if any one of those ships fired one shot in our direction, sink them—eliminate them.

We descended to about fifty feet and saw several ships with men working like they would on a typical fishing boat. They were throwing out nets, working the lines, and bringing in fish, but then we also saw about four fishing ships where the men were standing on the deck at attention. As we flew closer, we could see that while they had fishing equipment, it was neatly stacked on the deck and clean as a whistle. They had divers over the side, who, we assumed, were tapping into the cable and carrying out the espionage. We made several passes over the fleet and took dozens of photographs.

We returned to Iceland; then I returned to Norfolk, Virginia, where I briefed the admiral. The admiral took the photographs to Washington, DC, and that was the last I heard about the Russian fishing fleet.

I returned to Norfolk and had been there about six weeks when the admiral came to me again and said, "Conter, I have orders to send you to Fort Bragg, North Carolina, and you're going to attend special forces training school. After you complete the training, you're going to be a survival officer." I replied, "Yes, sir" and then left Norfolk for Fort Bragg, where I became a part of the very first US Special Forces training class.

I think this is an appropriate time to mention that while I am confident many of the events I participated in while serving as an intelligence officer would make for stimulating reading, I cannot and will not discuss certain aspects of my life. Most of the missions I participated in simply cannot and will not be addressed. Even though this is my first and only memoir, most of those missions were, and remain, highly classified, even after sixty to sixty-five years. There were missions I was involved with that were deemed classified for life, and that is where they stay with me. That said, I will make one statement: some people had to be eliminated for peaceful purposes; they were, and those situations will and must forever remain classified.

I must say that my time as an intelligence officer was one of the most fascinating periods of my life. I was active with three branches of the United States of America's most elite intelligence-gathering entities, and I can say without reservation that I am proud to have served with so many amazing people.

14

SPECIAL FORCES TRAINING

BY THE EARLY 1950S, I thought I had met some pretty special people, and I had, but when I began my training with the US Special Forces, I had the honor to be in the presence of some pretty amazing people, starting with the man who commanded the very first class of special forces trainees, Colonel Aaron Bank.

For those who do not know much about the US Special Forces, they were officially formed in 1952, initially under the US Army Psychological Warfare Division headed by then-brigadier general Robert A. McClure. Special Operations Command was formed by the US Army Psychological Warfare Center, which was activated in May of 1952 and was commanded by Colonel Aaron Bank. Its formation coincided with the establishment of the Psychological Warfare School, which is now known as the John F. Kennedy Special Warfare Center and School (IBP USA, 2016).

Colonel Bank was no ordinary guy. He had spent much of his youth traveling in Europe. Fluent in French and, to a lesser extent, in German, Bank lived and worked in Europe, including a stint as the head lifeguard at a posh resort in Biarritz, France. He joined the Army in 1939, but as an older officer, he was precluded from an active combat role, and he was assigned as a training officer to a railroad battalion at Fort Polk, Louisiana, when the United States entered the war. Happening upon a notice for volunteers with language capability, he volunteered for the OSS and was assigned to the Special Operations branch. He soon found himself in England, leading a three-person Jedburgh team behind the lines in occupied France after D-Day (Bank, 1986).

On the night of July 31, 1944, Bank parachuted into France, where he and his team provided support for two resistance factions, the Gaullist forces *Francaises de l'Intérieur* and communist *Francs-Tieurs et Partisans,* as the two groups harassed the retreating Germans and battled each other for supremacy in the liberated towns that the Germans had evacuated. For six weeks, Bank and his team rotated between the various partisan groups training them in guerrilla warfare (Bank, 1995).

Bank found himself back in London as the leader of Operation *Iron Cross*, a mission to insert five Americans and nearly two hundred ex-German Army volunteers into the Inn Valley in Austria to create havoc in the German rear and ultimately attempt to capture Adolph Hitler and other high-ranking Nazis from what was thought to be their redoubt (stronghold) in Berchtesgaden. Bank trained his team to a razor's edge only to have the mission aborted in April 1945 when the Seventh Army rolled into Austria and Bavaria, and the Third Reich collapsed. With the end of *Iron Cross,* Bank volunteered to join the OSS in the Far East and soon found himself in Kunming, China (Bank, 1995).

Bank's new missions included training a two-hundred-man company of Vietnamese soldiers formerly in the French Army and three French officers to lead them on a raid against an Army-level Japanese headquarters on the Red River near Hanoi. This mission was canceled in July 1945 when it was determined that the Viet Minh would not allow the entrance of the French back into the country. He subsequently parachuted with a nine-man team into Laos to search for internees and prisoners of war and eventually made his way to Hanoi and accompanied Ho Chi Minh to Hue. In October 1945, the OSS was disbanded and all the teams recalled. Bank returned to the regular Army at the end of the war (Bank, 1976).

In 1951, he served as the executive officer of the 187th Regimental Combat Team in Korea. Promoted to colonel, he was reassigned to the Army's psychological warfare staff in the Pentagon, under the direction of Brigadier General Robert A. McClure. Joined by Lieutenant Colonel Russell Volckmann and Colonel Wendell Fertig, World War II veterans who led guerrilla units in the Philippines, Bank formulated the doctrine and principles that became the foundation of today's special forces (Finlayson, 2006).

As I said, Colonel Bank was no ordinary guy.

When I arrived at Fort Bragg and walked into my first training class, I immediately spotted an old friend, Herbie Brucker, who was not only an attendee at the school but was helping Colonel Bank develop and run the school's entire training program. Like Bank, Herbie Brucker was no ordinary guy.

Herbert R. Brucker was a radioman of a three-man special operations executive team that operated in France before D-Day. Unlike the OSS, Jedburgh, and operational groups (OG), British special operations had been working behind German lines since late 1940. Technical Sergeant Four (T/4) Brucker was detailed to the SOE in England as "Herbert E-54" because he had been raised from infancy in the bilingual Alsace and Lorraine provinces of France. On May 26, 1944, Second Lieutenant "Albert Brunion" (codename Sacha) and Second Lieutenant Roger B. Henquet jumped into France to establish the Hermit circuit, replacing Prosper, which had been "rolled up" by the Germans. Their third teammate, Frenchman Henri Fucs, a surgeon recovering from a bicycle injury, joined them later. Having attributed the majority of the Hermit team success to "Albert Brunion," Brucker was awarded the Distinguished Service Cross (Brisco, 2006).

After returning to England in September 1944, Herbie, who had been promoted to the rank of second lieutenant, agreed to other OSS assignments in the Far East and was then promoted to first lieutenant and ended up doing a variety of missions in Burma and China.

My understanding is that when Herbie was in Burma, he served in one of the most notable OSS units, Detachment 101, which was dropped behind enemy lines, where they conducted a series of guerrilla operations to identify targets for Allied airstrikes, rescue downed pilots, and disrupt supply lines.

After the war, Herbie served with counterintelligence; he was then ordered to Fort Bragg, North Carolina, where he joined the Eighty-Second Airborne Division and was promoted to the rank of captain. Herbie was at Fort Bragg when the North Koreans invaded the South on June 25, 1950.

As the commander of Headquarters Company, Second Battalion, 505th Infantry, Herbie learned that the Department of the Army was seeking volunteers for US Special Forces, and that was when Colonel Bank made Brucker the acting S-2 (security) responsible for processing all special forces security clearances—a major job—and the chief of clandestine operations training (Bank, 1995).

During the Korean War, Herbie was still actively conducting various top-secret operations, which was how we first met, and I am sure my having known and worked with Herbie in Korea had something to do with my assignment to complete the Army special forces training, especially since I was the only naval officer in the class.

Another interesting fact about Herbie is that he designed and created the signature green beret that has been worn with tremendous pride by the special forces' Army members since 1953.

I do not believe the military could have picked a better person to run the school than Colonel Bank, nor do I believe that Colonel Bank could have found anyone better to assist him than Herbie Brucker. They were a great team, and, more importantly, they were great teachers.

Colonel Bank acknowledged Herbie's contribution to the special forces training when he stated for the record, "We had no precedent, no manuals. Herb Brucker and I developed our own program—the Army left us alone" (Zimmerman, 2012).

As I said, Herbie Brucker was no ordinary guy.

Colonel Bank assembled a squad of officers and NCOs for his first class of special forces recruits. He did not want raw recruits. He wanted the best troops in the Army, and he got them: former OSS officers, former airborne troops, ex-Rangers and combat veterans of World War II and Korea, and me, US Navy Lieutenant Louis Conter, the only non-Army member of the class.

It did not matter to my classmates that I was Navy; the only thing that mattered was that we all worked as a team during our training.

Every day was tough. We were out of the rack at the crack of dawn, and it was class after class after class. We did physical training every day with push-ups, sit-ups, and running, lots of running. We were even dropped off at a base camp near Gannett Peak in Wyoming, where we were given a seventy-pound backpack, a map, and some field rations (freeze-dried food) and told to climb to the top of the mountain.

As I mentioned, since everyone else in attendance was Army, they were all OSS officers, which meant they had all had parachute training. Well, First Lieutenant Charles Norton came up to me and said, "Lou, we have all jumped, but you have never jumped from a plane, have you?" I said I had taken a class in flight school in 1942, but I had never actually jumped from a plane before. I had never had to because I had always had good planes, so I could always fly them in and land them.

After Charles finished laughing, he said, "Well, we will have to take you over and have you jump." So they took me over to the tarmac and gave me a few pointers. Charles gave me a pair of boots, threw me a parachute, and took me out to a plane.

We took off and reached the correct elevation (which I think must have been around fifteen hundred feet above ground level). I hooked my static line to the central cable that ran the length of the plane, and the next thing I knew, I was out of the door.

If you have never jumped from a plane before, it is like you are going nowhere fast. All you are doing is falling from the sky to the ground. Once your parachute deploys, you experience a few seconds of intense deceleration. You probably hit around three to four Gs, and then eventually your speed slows from about 120 miles per hour to about seventeen miles per hour. When you hit the ground, the important thing is that you relax your body and roll.

After I landed, Charles came up to me and said, "Great job, Lou; now, let's get back in the plane and do it again." So we did. During the second jump, I again used the static line, jumped from the plane, floated to the earth, hit the ground, and rolled. After I landed, Charles came up to me and once again said, "Great job, Lou; now, let's get back in the plane and do it again." So we did.

For the third jump, however, I did not get to use the static line; instead, I had to pull the parachute's ripcord, so I jumped from the plane, pulled my ripcord, floated to the earth, hit the ground, and rolled. By then, I think that the Army guys realized that I was starting to enjoy jumping out of planes, so that was it for the day.

I know that jumping out of planes is not something that most naval people would embrace, but I enjoyed jumping and the feeling of freedom that came with it, even if it was nothing like the thrill of flying a plane. Altogether, I jumped five times and loved it each time.

I think it probably surprised the guys in the Army that an aviator would enjoy jumping out of a perfectly good plane, but it was a requirement for the course, so I had to do what everyone else was doing, or I wouldn't have deserved to be there.

An interesting side note on First Lt. Charles Norton: after having enlisted in the Army in 1944, Norton ended up spending thirty-five years in the Army and had an extremely distinguished career. Norton's awards and decorations include the Combat Infantryman's Badge, three Legions of Merit, two Bronze Star Medals, one Bronze Star Medal with Valor device, the Joint Service Commendation Medal, seven Air Medals, the Vietnamese Cross of Gallantry with gold and silver stars, the Army General Staff Identification Badge, the Excellence in Competition Badge (rifle), the Good Conduct Medal (three awards), the Order of the Knights of the Finnish White, the US Army Parachutist Badge, and eleven service medals. After his retirement in 1981, he continued his association with special forces as a member, later president, and now as president emeritus of the Special Forces Association Chapter XI in Washington, DC. He established procedures ensuring chapter members attend all interments of special forces members (active duty, retired, officer, or enlisted) at Arlington National Cemetery. Additionally, he serves as liaison with the First Special Service Force Association, attending their annual reunions (US Army, 2011).

In 2011, Colonel Charles W. Norton was inducted as a Distinguished Member of the Special Forces Regiment. Like Bank and Brucker, Colonel Charles W. Norton was . . . that's right: no ordinary guy. There were a lot of "no ordinary guys" in that first special forces class, many of whom went on to have amazing careers in the military and after they retired from the service and entered the civilian world.

Today's special forces training is much, much different than that very first training class. Our program ran for approximately six months; now, the qualification course consists of six phases and runs a little over a year. While much has changed, there is still a common thread that runs through every person who serves, and has served, not just in special forces but also in the military in general and the stewardship of being a soldier. For those who serve—especially in a specialized unit such as the Army Special Forces (Rangers, Night Stalkers, and Green Berets), the Marine Corps Special Forces (Raiders or Force RECON), the Air Force Special Tactics teams (Pararescuemen, combat controllers, and weathermen), or the Navy SEAL teams—members of these units know that it is an honor to put on the uniform of their respective branch of service and serve our great nation.

Special forces units are deployed worldwide. They are known for their humanitarian assistance and training of indigenous forces, as well as their direct action and special reconnaissance missions. Special forces soldiers live up to their motto: *de oppresso liber* (to free the oppressed). I can say, without hesitation, that I was honored to be one of the first men to attend special forces training and was so grateful to be in the presence of so many great men.

15

SURROUNDED BY GREATNESS

AFTER I COMPLETED SPECIAL forces training, the Navy sent me to E and E school, which was escape and evade training. The class roster was represented by every branch of the service and by all officers, except for one civilian. Much like special forces training, the E and E school I attended was filled with amazing people.

I knew going into training that once I had completed the four-month course, I would become one of two designed survival, escape and evasion, resistance, and espionage (SERE) officers for the US Navy, the other being Ed Profe, one of the first underwater demolition leaders of World War II, so I wanted to pick the brains of not only our instructors but the men in the class as well. When I walked into the class, I could not believe the quality of military men who filled the room. Old friends such as Charles Norton and Caesar Civitella were there (I will talk about Caesar shortly), and so were men with whom I would become lifelong friends. We had heroes in the group and men who were to become heroes. I can say without reservation that every member of this group went on to do something significant. Here are a few of my fellow classmates:

Joseph James Koontz—Joe's duty assignments included

teaching a wide variety of topics for an even wider variety of schools and in numerous countries. His awards and decorations include Legion of Merit (Combat Action), Silver Star, Bronze Star Medal, Air Medal, Combat Infantryman Badge, Philippine Liberation Medal, Philippine Presidential Unit Citation, Army Commendation Ribbon, Asiatic-Pacific Campaign Medal, Army of Occupation (Japan) Nat Def, NDSM 1st Oak Leaf Cluster, Decoration Government of Colombia, and six overseas bars (The US Army OCS Alumni Association, 2020). During the class, Joe held the rank of colonel.

John A. Kupsick—During World War II, John, who was a navigator of a B-17, was shot down over a French village during a mission. John and several crew members were taken to a safe hiding place, where they worked with the French underground for seven months until Allied troops retook the village from the Germans. Later in his career, he served as the vice commander of the Thirty-Ninth Air Division in Misawa, Japan, and did a five-year stint at the Pentagon with the Joint Chiefs of Staff (The Cottage Grove Sentinel, 2013). During the class, John held the rank of major.

Leon Newby Utter—Leon, who would go on to serve in Vietnam, was cited for his gallantry and intrepidity in action as the commanding officer, Second Battalion, Seventh Marines, First Marine Division (Rein), during his battalion's participation in a mission called Operation Harvest Moon. During the operation, he expertly led his battalion on extended search-and-destroy operations through areas in Quang Nam Province, which had been stubbornly controlled by the Viet Cong for an extended period (The Hall of Valor Project, 2020). I could go into detail about Leon's background and his heroics, but instead, I will recommend a book written on him by Lieutenant Colonel Alex Lee titled *Utter's Battalion*, which is a fascinating read. During the class, Leon held the rank of lieutenant colonel.

Bruce F. Meyers—Bruce commanded a rifle company in Korea (1951). He had a pivotal role in forming Force Recon, becoming the commanding officer of First Force Recon (1957), battalion commander of the Sixth Fleet Landing Force (1966), and commander of Special Landing Force Alpha aboard the LPH Iwo Jima. In Vietnam, Colonel Meyers commanded the Twenty-Sixth Marines at Khe Sanh during the Tet offensive in 1968. Upon his retirement from the Marines in 1970, Meyers passed the Virginia State Bar and then the Washington State Bar (Forcerecon, 2017). Bruce was the author of three amazing books: *Fortune Favors the Brave—The Story of First Force Recon*; *Reflections of a Grunt Marine*; and *Swift, Silent, and Deadly—Marine Amphibious Reconnaissance in the Pacific, 1942–1945* (Meyers, 2001). During the class, Bruce held the rank of lieutenant colonel.

Joseph Z. Taylor—Joe served for a little more than two months with the US Marines First Force Reconnaissance Company and was promoted to the rank of major and then became the commanding officer of the US Marines Second Force Reconnaissance Company. During his tenure with Force Reconnaissance Company, the Marines helped with the development and refinement of submarine insertions/extractions techniques, low-level static line and military free-fall parachute insertion, the closed-circuit SCUBA procedures, and the initial deep reconnaissance capability within the Department of Defense (Fleet Marine Force Reconnaissance, 2020). During the class, Joe held the rank of captain.

Charles Maze "Bill" Simpson—Bill was one of the last of that rare breed of soldier-scholar who went into special forces early on and stayed. He was representative of the classic Chinese ideal of the warrior, equally at home wielding a sword or a pen (Assembly, 2002). Bill was one of those guys who was tough and smart. In 1952, during the Korean War, he was the commander of K Company, Seventeenth Infantry, Seventh Division. Later, Bill attended Harvard, where he received a master's in public administration and then went on to teach in the social science department at West Point. Then, following his tour at West Point, Bill became commander of the First Special Forces Group in Okinawa. During his military career, he received the Silver Star; three Bronze Stars for Valor; a Purple Heart; four Legions of Merit; an Army Commendation Ribbon; five Air Medals; Korean, Japanese, Taiwanese, Vietnamese, Thai, and Indonesian jump wings; and two awards of the Combat Infantryman Badge for Korea and Vietnam (The West Point Connection, 1990). Like many others in the class, Bill also wrote an excellent book on his life, *Inside the Green Berets: The First Thirty Years*. During the class, Bill held the rank of colonel.

William R. Whorton—William joined the Navy in 1945, remained on active duty until 1946, and then reentered the Navy during the Korean War and flew with Patrol Squadron 11. He served as a flight instructor for advanced flight training. Following the Korean War, Whorton had various assignments, including as the commanding officer of a squadron assigned to Vietnam, the operations officer for the Seventh Fleet, the staffer for the chief of naval operations, and a defense attaché to Uruguay. During his time in the military, William received various honors and medals including the Bronze Star, Meritorious Service Medal, Combat Air Medal, American Campaign Medal, World War II Victory Medal, National Defense Service Medal, Korea Service Medal, Vietnam Service Medal, and United Nations Service Medal. On November 7, 2007, he was honored with induction into the Patriots Hall of Honor (Butler, 2007). During the class, William held the rank of lieutenant commander.

John Clapper—John was an aviator and, by all accounts, a pretty good one. Clapper was a Silver Star recipient for gallantry in action while serving with the Firth Air Force and in action against the enemy in the Southwest Pacific Theater of Operations during World War II during his stint with the US Army Air Force (The Hall of Valor Project, 2020). It was fun to visit with John, and we shared many tall tales of our lives as aviators. During the class, John held the rank of captain.

Herman Hansen—Herman became a World War II Marine Corps Ace for shooting down five enemy aircraft in aerial combat and assisting in shooting down a sixth, and for his extraordinary heroism and distinguished service in his profession as commanding officer and pilot of Marine Fighting Squadron 112 (VMF-112). He embarked from the USS *Bennington* (CV-20) in aerial combat against enemy Japanese forces in the vicinity of Amami-O-Shima, Japan, on April 12, 1945. Leading a flight of twelve carrier-based fighter planes against a numerically superior force of hostile aircraft, Herman skillfully shot down three enemy fighters and aided his squadron in destroying or seriously damaging the entire formation. After returning to base, he again led his flight in destroying a formation of enemy dive bombers that were attempting suicide attacks on our surface forces. A superb leader and airman, Herman contributed to the destruction of twenty enemy aircraft and the infliction of crippling damage on six others, returning his entire flight to base intact and undamaged. His gallant fighting spirit and courageous devotion to duty were in keeping with the US naval service's highest traditions, and for his action, Herman was awarded the Navy Cross (The Hall of Valor Project, 2020). During the class, Herman held the rank of major.

Gene E. Taft—Gene excelled in many sports in high school and was recruited to play football for Oregon State in Corvallis. Gene was a great football player for the Beavers. In 1950, he finished second on the team in rushing yards behind his backfield running mate, Sam Baker (who had a fifteen-year career in the National Football League). Gene also finished second on

the team in passing yards and returned punts, was the leading
kickoff returner, and even had a seventy-nine-yard return for
a touchdown that stood as an Oregon State University record
for decades. Gene was a distinguished graduate of the US Air
Force ROTC program and, in 1954, entered the Air Force. Upon
completion of pilot training, he served thirty years in several key
leadership positions around the world. During his combat tour
in Vietnam, Gene, flying the F4 Phantom, was credited with
shooting down an enemy MIG aircraft. His many awards and
decorations include the Silver Star, Bronze Star, Distinguished
Flying Cross with Two Oak Leaf Clusters, Air Medal with Eleven
Oak Leaf Clusters, and Republic of Vietnam Gallantry Cross
(Legacy, 2015). During the class, Gene held the rank of captain.

Dr. Paul H. Nesbitt—Paul was the only civilian in the group,
and from 1949 through 1958, he was a desert survival expert at
the Arctic, Desert, and Tropic Information Center at the Maxwell Air Force Base in Alabama and worked with the US Army
Air Force, training in desert warfare research. Paul had earned
his PhD at the University of Chicago and was an anthropology
professor at the Air University, Maxwell Air Force Base in Alabama (Smith, 2002). In 1959, Paul authored a book appropri-
ately called *The Survival Book*, which was pretty much based on
what he had already known about survival and what he learned
in our E and E class. In 1967, Paul became chairman and anthropology professor at the University of Alabama, so he was
basically a real-life Indiana Jones.

Caesar J. Civitella—Caesar, whom I stayed in contact with
until the time of his death, which came in 2017, like so many in
this early E and E class, had a very distinguished military career,
and his accomplishments could fill a book; he probably would
have written one if almost every aspect of life had not been
classified. During World War II, Caesar helped French resistance
fighters and Italian partisans fight Nazis and fascists when he

served with the OSS, the military's first joint special operations organization, led by William "Wild Bill" Donovan, an Army two-star general who helped create the OSS during World War II to perform commando missions.

Caesar's first mission was called Operation Dragoon, which was part of the Allied invasion of Provence (Southern France). Working with the French Maquis resistance group, Civitella's fourteen-man OSS operational team captured nearly thirty-eight hundred enemy soldiers and thirty Nazi officers. Nine months later, after serving on aerial resupply missions that earned him the Air Medal, Civitella and another team dropped behind enemy lines, this time in northern Italy. They worked with Italian resistance forces to prevent the Nazis and fascists from destroying infrastructure as they retreated and to capture Italian fascist dictator Benito Mussolini.

Once on the ground, Caesar and his team traveled by horse and sled through the mountains. They were carrying gold to pay the people who had Mussolini. By the time they arrived behind enemy lines, however, Italian partisans had already captured and killed Mussolini. Still, Caesar and his team remained in the field for another month until the Germans surrendered. He earned a Bronze Star (Tip of the Spear, 2008).

After the war, Caesar compiled after-action reports for one of the most famous members of the OSS, Commander John Ford, whom most will remember as an Academy Award-winning director of the films *The Informer*, *Stagecoach*, and *The Grapes of Wrath* and an Oscar winner for Best Documentary during World War II for the films *Battle of Midway* and *December 7*. Ford is also remembered as someone who just happened to be on the Island of Midway during the Battle of Midway (Tip of the Spear, 2008).

In 1946, Caesar left the Army to attend the University of Pennsylvania, but the call to action was too strong, and he reenlisted again in 1947. In 1952, Second Lt. Civitella was among the first men recruited into the new special forces program, where he was one of the first to train Green Berets. After he helped develop the special forces doctrine, Caesar shipped out in 1961 for the first of his three tours of duty as a soldier in Vietnam. On August 31, 1964, Caesar, a major at the time, retired from the Army. Less than twenty-four hours later, he joined the CIA and was assigned to the agency's Air Branch "to support clandestine service air requirements" (Tip of the Spear, 2008).

Caesar wrapped up his career at MacDill Air Force Base in Tampa, serving as a CIA liaison to the commands that would eventually become SOCom and US Central Command, which oversees US military efforts in the Middle East and Southwest Asia. He retired on August 31, 1983, and was awarded the CIA's Intelligence Medal of Merit (Green, 2018).

I shared earlier that I cannot write about certain things in my career because they were classified and remain so still to this day. Caesar never wrote a book about his life because just about everything he did during his career was, and remains, classified. He was America's James Bond, and I was honored to have him as a friend. During the class, Caesar held the rank of captain.

There were thirty-one of us in that first class, and I could probably write about the exploits of every single member of our class roster. Each man has a story, and I can assure you that everyone from our group went on to make a significant contribution to our US military. These were men who cared about their country and their fellow countrymen and -women.

While the course lasted approximately four months, I had gained valuable information that would allow me to train the men under my command efficiently and effectively, but more importantly, I had made several friends with whom I stayed in contact long after my service to our country had concluded. These were men who defended our county so that we could live under the umbrella of freedom.

I know I keep repeating myself when I say it was an absolute honor to be in the presence of such greatness, but it was. My military career was wonderful, and in most of the situations I found myself in, I always seemed to be surround by good people; maybe that was one of the reasons I was able to survive my time in the military: I had extraordinary people all around me.

16

SERE Training

THE NAVY'S FIRST SURVIVAL, escape and evasion, resistance to interrogation, and espionage training took place at Camp Mackall, which is right next to Fort Bragg. The Army still uses Camp Mackall to help train today's special forces members. The training program was called Operation Tenderfoot, and it was SERE training for the Navy before there was SERE training for the Navy. In essence, the Navy worked in conjunction with the Army for its SERE training before the Navy's SERE school became developed and functional.

My old friend from special forces training, Herbie Brucker, helped set up the class. I helped Herbie teach courses and run the program. The lessons learned at the E and E school proved beneficial to the Navy personnel, so we were given the green light to develop an entire curriculum and training protocol. The course was designed for Navy pilots and their crewmen. We would teach attendees how to survive, evade, resist, and escape the enemy if they were shot down behind enemy lines.

Let me start by saying that today's SERE training is nothing like it was in the 1950s. Our mission was to train pilots and aircrewmen how to live in the jungle if they got shot down. We taught them how to escape and evade, how to live in a prison camp, and how not to break under interrogation. We were training our pilots and aircrewman to survive in dangerous situations. Much has changed since the early 1950s, and I am sure there will be members of our modern military who will read the information in this chapter and roll their eyes. I would offer this piece of advice to those folks: Keep in mind, we were the first of our kind. Our principles and training may seem crude and rudimentary by today's standards, but as with technology, time improves almost everything, including training.

During WWII, the US Navy discovered that 75 percent of pilots who had been shot or forced down came down alive, yet barely 5 percent of them survived because they could not swim or find sustenance in the water or on remote islands (Swim Swam, 2018). Having been shot down twice and having had to survive these water crashes, I valued the training that aviators and their crew members were provided for this specific situation, and by the time I took control of the SERE training, the Navy had already started to adjust its training priorities.

Training programs were developed to ensure that pilot trainees could swim (requiring cadets to swim one mile and dive fifty feet underwater to escape bullets and suction from sinking aircraft) since this ability was an essential survival skill for Navy pilots. Soon, the training was expanded to include submerged aircraft escape (Swim Swam, 2018).

The Korean War showed that traditional notions about captives during wartime were no longer valid—the Koreans (with Chinese backing) ignored the Geneva Convention regarding the treatment of POWs, and captured American soldiers were not prepared for what they faced. This was especially true of American airmen, who took the brunt of mistreatment because of their hated bombardments and their prestige among soldiers. The Koreans were very interested in the propaganda value of their American captives, and their new methods (with those of the Chinese) for gaining compliance, extracting confessions, and gathering information proved unnervingly successful against US soldiers (Carlson, 2002).

North Korea had approximately twenty known POW camps located throughout the country where servicemen underwent some of the most brutal conditions any human could endure. Suspected brainwashing was a convenient answer to why so many of our men collaborated with communist interrogators. The techniques used to exploit POWs were unprecedented from previous US war involvement. Propaganda was used as a method to manipulate the truth, and it proved to be effective in swaying world opinion as to the treatment of captured Americans and allies (Daland, 2011).

Throughout communist Korea, the prisoners faced brutal torture, random genocide, lack of food, absence of medical aid, and inhuman treatment, which became a familiar daily struggle of survival. Under these conditions, men committed acts inconsistent with their character.

Every one of the prisoners was forced to deal with the external and internal pressures of confinement, for which they were not adequately trained. Yet Washington was perplexed at the number of men who collaborated with the enemy or conducted acts against fellow POWs. An investigation took place into these alleged accusations and became validated, so a plan was needed to prevent this from reoccurring in future conflicts (Daland, 2011).

The Navy knew it had to do a better job preparing pilots and flight crews for the potential challenge of being held captive, and SERE training was now the wave of the future.

One of the first things I did was develop a document called "The Will to Live," the foundation of which was in survival psychology. Survival experts have long recognized the importance of the will to live. Physicians note it is crucial for a patient's recovery; chaplains and other clergy discourse about it; social workers speak of it in the adjustment of the aged and others. The will to survive is usually regarded as either a mysterious force beyond human understanding or something you can maintain by sheer willpower.

From the survival experience of hundreds of armed forces personnel downed during World War II and the Korean conflict, simple survival principles have been developed that dispel any mystery concerning the will to live. As for the value of sheer willpower, any well-trained, well-disciplined military person in good physical condition stands an excellent chance of surviving an emergency in peacetime or finding him- or herself suddenly behind enemy lines during wartime.

There are eight simple guidelines for survival:

S - Size up the situation.

U - Undue haste makes waste—have patience.

R - Remember where you are.

V - Vanquish fear and panic.

I – Improvise.

V - Value living.

A - Act like those around you—live with the natives.

L - Live through being well trained—learn basic skills.

1. Size up the situation.

Always be prepared for trouble, even when you are close to home. Remember, even at home, you can't think if you aren't calm. One person stated, "I attribute my safe return to my preparation, both mental and equipment-wise. Going down couldn't happen to me, but I was not going to take any chances. So I prepared myself, and I believe it was wise and paid off."

Take a minute or two; look the situation over, figure out what to do, check over the equipment you have at hand (no matter how little), decide on a course of action, and formulate a plan. If you are under enemy control, put yourself in his shoes; watch his habits and routine. Use reason.

2. Undue haste makes waste.

Don't be too eager to escape. Haste makes you get careless and impatient, and you take unnecessary risks. Hold your temper and face the facts. Watch for these signs: you begin to swear, you stop thinking, or you get mad. When this happens, it is time to stop, take a deep breath, and relax. Then start over again.

3. Remember where you are.

There is the story about the soldier successfully evading when a woman started whistling "Tipperary" (which was a popular marching song among soldiers in the First World War). Quoting the eventual evader, "I'm not sure just what I did, but it gave me away." He no doubt started whistling along with her, and if he had not been an enemy, he would not have known the song.

Another time, a German officer came out into a prison compound and ordered all units to fall in by crew, and one crew did so, from pilot to tail gunner. Remember where you are. Doing what comes naturally may be a tip-off that you do not belong there.

4. Vanquish your fear and panic.

Everyone in a dangerous situation feels fear. It's normal and natural, so don't be ashamed of it. It is nature's way of giving you an extra shot of energy when you need it. Find things to do and keep yourself busy. A careful look at the situation often reduces fear and prevents panic. Fear and panic probably account for more unnecessary casualties than any other cause. Below are two different true cases, one ending tragically, the other happily.

Example one—If this man had been able to stop and think, he probably would have escaped. His parachute caught in a tree, and he was suspended head down with his left foot tangled in the webbing. Unfortunately, the pilot had touched an anthill, and biting insects immediately swarmed over him. Apparently, in desperation, he pulled his gun and fired five rounds into the webbing holding his feet. When he failed in breaking the harness by shooting at it, he placed the last shot in his head and thus took his own life.

Example two—This man was injured and unable to move. Not knowing what to do, he decided to kill all the bugs around him. There were a lot of spiders, the big ones that do not hurt humans, so he killed the flies and gave them to the spiders to eat. He was of sound mind and only mildly shocked when rescued. He survived because he stopped fear from taking over his thoughts.

Below are some ways to keep fear at bay in dangerous or captive situations:

A. Don't run.
B. When you investigate, you will find many of your fears are not real.
C. Realize that pain adds to panic and keeps you from thinking.

D. Recognize that it is the loneliness that is getting to you, not the whole situation.

E. Planning your escape will keep your mind busy.

F. Form a workable plan and stick to it until you find a better one.

G. Groups of two to four are the best whenever possible. In this size group, fewer men report thoughts of suicide than do those in larger groups or going it alone.

H. If you must survive alone, you have only yourself to deal with. You can make your own plans and count on your own resources.

I. Observe carefully, like an outsider, what is happening to you.

J. Read or write.

K. Don't be ashamed of your religious or philosophical beliefs. This does not mean that you can take a passive attitude. Miracles work best for those who prepare carefully and who do all they can to save themselves.

5. Improvise.

Make a special effort to take care of yourself if you need something you don't have. After all, a boot is just a cover for your foot, and there are other ways to cover it. Be willing to put up with new and unpleasant thoughts—not necessarily harmful but unpleasant. For example, some things are worse than bad air. An aviator crashed near Pyongyang and lived in a cave with two native Koreans for twenty-three days. The aviator could not stand the air's smell in the cave and decided he had to leave. He left the cave and was soon captured. The area was surrounded and searched until the two Koreans were found. The aviator caused all three men to be captured because he did not like the cave's smell.

Another story makes the same point. A man was offered a popular native dish, something his mother never made. Some men would almost starve before eating the food. There was a soup made from a lamb's head with its eyes floating around it. The first time the man was offered the dish, he refused it. Several months later, when a new man arrived, the first man sat next to him so he could eat what the new man was going to refuse to eat. Don't be afraid to try new foods.

6. Value living.

A real plan for and hope to escape lessens pain and improves your chances of survival. Take your mind off the present and think of a better future. Hunger, cold, fatigue, and the like lower efficiency and stamina, which results in carelessness, leading to capture. They also break a man's spirit so that he just gives up. Knowing this will help you be especially careful. You will even realize that your low morale results from your physical condition and not the danger. The constant goal of getting out alive will help you keep your chin up and make the extra effort. Concentrating on the time after you get out alive will help you value living now.

7. Act like those around you.

When in Rome, do as the Romans do; otherwise, you'll stick out like a sore thumb. Failure to accept the customs of the locals makes you conspicuous and likely to be detected. Modesty is alright, but do not carry it too far in the wrong place. There were German guards at a railway station. An American who had eluded his captors had an urgent need to urinate. The only restroom was an exposed one in front of the station. The American felt too embarrassed to relieve himself in front of all the passersby, so he walked throughout the entire town, occasionally stopping to inquire if someone had a restroom available. He was taken prisoner a short while later.

8. Live by being well trained.

The best survival insurance you can have is to ensure that the training is so thorough that it becomes automatic. People may panic and be confused if they do not know what to do. Keep yourself briefed.

What to do: learn the best emergency procedures and practice them both as an individual and as a team.

A. Rehearse in your mind what you would do in various emergency situations.
B. Work on the training you have at hand. It may mean your life.
C. Keep informed about present situations.
D. Recognize when someone has to take leadership.

Time and time again, the experiences of American troops who suffered ordeals of communist POW camps during the Korean War and the ample testimony to the importance of the code of conduct have shown that American prisoners who revealed nothing more than their name, rank, serial number, and date of birth were far better off than those who showed a willingness to talk "just a little."

I will discuss the code of conduct later in this chapter, but for now, I would like readers to know that effective instruction on the code of conduct will do much to prevent the recurrence of our unfortunate experiences in communist prisons in Korea. Not a single American prisoner is known to have escaped from a permanent POW compound and successfully made his way to the friendly control during the Korean War. Some American

prisoners were guilty of breaches of conduct, such as collabora-
tion or mistreatment of fellow prisoners. More than one-third of
US POWs died in captivity.

Human beings are and will remain the essential element in
war. People, not machines, win or lose the battle. Machines cannot wage war; they can only increase human effectiveness. The
importance of the individual increases with the complexity of
the weapons he or she must employ. Humanity's significance
will advance until we have weapons that can think and improvise, meet reverses with resolution, match hardship and danger
with devotion and courage, and carry on to final victory. There
is no such weapon on the horizon. This was said in a talk by
General Lyman L. Lemnitzer.

The importance of physical fitness in rigorous field training
is too often minimized in this automation era of machines. We
tend to forget that more than one-third of the world is covered
by tropical jungle in which many of our most complicated weapons and equipment are useless. Some of the most sensitive potential trouble spots in the world are jungle areas. In such areas,
success in battle depends almost entirely on the individual soldier's training and physical and mental stamina.

Many American soldiers went into World War II with little
jungle training and paid dearly for it. As they were physically
unprepared for the rigors of fighting and existing in the jungle,
fear of the unknown often shattered their fighting spirit.

Lieutenant General Robert L. Eichelberger, who commanded
American units in the desperate fighting at Buna, New Guinea,
reflected on this in his book *Our Jungle Road to Tokyo*.

The first thing I found was that troops in the frontline positions had no trustworthy knowledge of Japanese positions. Our
patrols were dazed by the hazards of swamp and jungle; they were
unwilling to undertake the patrolling which alone could safe-
guard their own interests. To get accurate information was almost

impossible, and yet, men die if orders are based on incorrect information.

I'm inclined to believe that the men were more frightened by the jungle than by the Japanese. It was the terror of the new and the unknown. There is nothing pleasant about sinking into a foul-smelling bog up to your knees. There is nothing enjoyable about lying in a trench half-submerged with tropical rain that quickly turns a trickling brook into a raging debris-filled river. Jungle noises were strange to most Americans, and in the moist hot darkness, the rustling of small animals in the bush was easily misinterpreted as the stealthy approach of the enemy.

The threat of nuclear weapons in modern war has brought sweeping changes in today's combat organization, fighting equipment, and tactical doctrines. On the automatic and the atomic battlefield, units and individuals will be separated and dispersed over wide frontages to avoid the formation of lucrative targets. More so than ever before, the fighters in the frontline are likely to find themselves cut off from their parent organization, suddenly isolated in a strange and lonely sector of the battlefield, perhaps behind enemy lines, possibly in enemy hands. The naval aviator or Air Force pilot and/or crew member will find themselves down many miles inside enemy territory, walking. We must remember that we speak of a soldier because any bird man without a plane becomes a foot soldier. More planning time must be devoted to our military personnel's psychological preparation to meet and overcome these conditions.

We must ensure that our soldiers are trained in techniques for avoiding capture. If it cannot possibly be avoided, they must be prepared to survive the rigors of enemy captivity. We must strengthen their will to resist interrogation, escape from enemy captivity, and avoid recapture once they are free.

President Eisenhower underscored the necessity for this type of training when he prescribed a code of conduct for men and women fighting for America. If imbued adequately with the spirit of the code, every member of the armed forces will be readily measured to the expected standard. The code of conduct is an excellent foundation for building the training program as it covers all aspects of behavior in enemy territory: survival, invasion, escape, and resistance to enemy interrogation. Instruction in these subjects cannot be integrated entirely into other training but must be presented individually, and adequate training time should be allotted to all armed forces personnel.

Total fitness for survival includes technical fitness, mental and emotional fitness, and physical fitness. If any of these attributes are lacking, survival effectiveness suffers proportionately. Without technical fitness, a person lacks the knowledge and skills to survive. Without mental and emotional fitness, he or she lacks the knowledge and will to survive. Without physical fitness, a person lacks the strength and endurance to survive. The physically fit individual enjoys a feeling of well-being and confidence in his or her ability to handle any emergency. A person's ability to accomplish a mission is improved because he or she has the strength and determination to avoid capture and, if captured, to resist efforts to break his or her will and lessen the desire to escape. Additionally, a physically capable person can exploit any opportunity to escape and, after escaping, can endure severe hardship until that person can make his or her way home.

Training is continually mentioned in any discussion of invasion and survival. Training gives experience, and from experience, a person gains forethought, ability, and efficiency. Lessons learned from experience are far more effective than theoretical lessons. Training during peacetime can be helpful, but no amount of training can make up for lack of personal determination. Training will help enormously if you have willpower, but you will not survive without determination.

The American fighting man or woman must be able to out-fight and outfox the enemy. Without tough, realistic training, there is little hope for survival on the isolated battlefield, evading behind enemy lines, or surviving the rigors of imprisonment in a POW compound.

The will to live is almost 100 percent of the battle in a survival situation. It was essential for us in the SERE training program to make sure that our people knew this and embraced the concept that having the will to live was key to their survival.

Soon after the Korean War ended, the Department of Defense initiated the Defense Advisory Committee on Prisoners of War to study and report on the problems, issues, and possible solutions regarding the Korean War POW fiasco. The committee's charter was to find a suitable approach for preparing our armed forces to deal with the combat and captivity environment. The committee's key recommendation was implementing a military code of conduct that embodied traditional American values as soldiers' moral obligations during combat and captivity. Underlying this code was the belief that imprisonment was thought of as an extension of the battlefield—a place where soldiers were expected to accept death as a possible duty (Daland, 2011).

In 1955, President Eisenhower issued Executive Order 10631, which stated, "Every member of the Armed Forces of the United States is expected to measure up to the standards embodied in the Code of Conduct while in combat or in captivity."

The authority for establishing the code of conduct, communication of intent, and assignment of responsibilities is outlined in the first three paragraphs of Executive Order 10631, which read as follows:

By virtue of the authority vested in me as President of the United States, and as Commander in Chief of the armed forces of the United States, I hereby prescribe the

Code of Conduct for Members of the Armed Forces of the United States which is attached to this order and hereby made a part thereof.

All members of the Armed Forces of the United States are expected to measure up to the standards embodied in this Code of Conduct while in combat or in captivity. To ensure achievement of these standards, members of the Armed Forces liable to capture shall be provided with specific training and instruction designed to equip them to better counter and withstand all enemy efforts against them and shall be fully instructed as to the behavior and obligations expected of them during combat or captivity.

The Secretary of Defense (and the Secretary of Transportation with respect to the Coast Guard except when it is serving as part of the Navy) shall take such action as is deemed necessary to implement this order and to disseminate and make the said Code known to all members of the Armed Forces of the United States (Eisenhower, 1955).

Here are the six articles of the code of conduct:

1. I am an American fighting in the forces which guard my country and our way of life. I am prepared to give my life in their defense.

2. I will never surrender of my own free will. If in command, I will never surrender my command members while still having the means to resist.

3. If I am captured, I will continue to resist by all means available. I will make every effort to escape and aid

others to escape. I will accept neither parole nor special favors from the enemy.

4. If I become a prisoner of war, I will keep faith with my fellow prisoners. I will give no information or take part in any action that might be harmful to my comrades. If I am senior, I will take command. If not, I will obey the lawful orders of those appointed over me and will back them up in every way.

5. Should I become a prisoner of war, when questioned, I am required to give name, rank, service number, and date of birth. I will evade answering further questions to the utmost of my ability. I will make no oral or written statements disloyal to my country and its allies or harmful to their cause.

6. I will never forget that I am an American who is fighting for freedom, responsible for my actions, and dedicated to the principles that made my country free. I will trust in my God and in the United States of America.

While it was accepted that the code of conduct would be taught to all US military personnel in their career, the US Armed Forces then began the process of training and implementing this directive, and the decree by President Eisenhower recognized the need to increase and intensify our SERE training.

Once we developed the curriculum and had our training philosophies and manuals in place, it was time to get the ball rolling and set up survival schools. We organized and ran the Cold Weather Survival School at NAS Brunswick, Maine, and the Jungle Schools at Panama, the Philippines, and Hawaii and held exercises at Stead AFB, Reno, Nevada; Canada; and Germany. When our people reported to SERE training, they were instructed in four training modules:

1. Survival—This was classroom work. We would teach our students how to live in the field by surviving off the land, building fires, catching and gathering food, and finding water, all while evading the enemy.

2. Evasion—Traveling behind enemy lines is a critical skill. If you are going to escape the enemy when you are in their territory, you must keep moving. Instructors who had very thick Russian accents would search the area looking for our downed aviators and their crews throughout the day and night.

3. Resistance—Students are either caught or have to turn themselves in to start the resistance phase of their training. Now, they are a captured POW and treated as such. Prisoners will be housed in a cell, just like a real POW, interrogated for hours at a time, just like an actual POW, and, yes, even beaten, just like a POW. While captured, our students' ultimate goal is not to give up any information during interrogations and not to be used as propaganda by the enemy.

4. Escape—The final aspect of training is the escape phase. The prison guards' goal is to make it as difficult as possible for any of the captives to break free from the camp. Students will be faced with having to deal with blaring loudspeakers that play repetitive, mind-numbing recordings; bright lights in the middle of the night; and, of course, water and food deprivation.

The intent of SERE training is not to be mean to or bully someone; the intent of SERE training is to prepare our military personnel with an understanding of how to survive a very, very bad situation. Ultimately, our survival guide became a fifty-page manual that was broken down into nine different sections.

Section one was our introduction, which discussed survival. Survival is usually defined as the ability to outlive, or continue to live despite, adverse circumstances. Each group tends to be assigned to the world's survival, a unique condition that may differ from that assigned to other individuals or groups, which may result in a misunderstanding; play precludes effective communication. It makes the development of principles and techniques difficult, if not impossible. The term "survival" is used for lack of a better word; at the same time, its dictionary definition is too limited and too general to indicate the true scope of military survival.

Section one included the definition of survival, military survival, military obligations, military survival medicine, survival situations, survival factors, limitation and exclusions, scope and approach, the survivor, the magnitude of the survival medicine problem, past deficiencies, and perspective.

I want to discuss survival and the survivor for a moment. The survivor is the most crucial member of his own rescue party, as well as the most important of the three components of the survival system (i.e., the person, his equipment, and proper techniques). It is axiomatic, then, that the maintenance of his health and well-being is essential to his successful survival. Survival is hard work, requiring peak mental and physical efficiency. Survivors are concurrently subjected to various hostile influences that combine to reduce efficiency via illness and injury. Survival is the ability to sustain life and retrain personal courage and determination in the midst of adverse circumstances that can be unfamiliar and, at their worst, extremely dangerous.

Anyone is only five minutes from a survival situation. Success or failure in a situation depends on the outlook of the individual and the absorption of factual material. Trust in rescue facilities should not replace the individual's ability to survive strictly on his own merits because rescue attempts may be ineffective, and during wartime, a search may be impossible to organize.

Could you survive for one week entirely on your own in, say, the Mojave Desert or the Sierra Mountains? Every civilian or military person could be put in this situation in everyday life. Prepare yourself for survival situations. One of the essential elements of survival is morale. Morale is defined as a prevailing mood and spirit conducive to willing and dependable performance, steady self-control, and courageous, determined conduct despite danger and privations, based on a conviction of being in the right and on the way to success.

The individual is likely to be in a state of shock in the initial phase of the survival situation, and his morale will probably be subjected to maximum pressure. This mental deterioration must be registered and resisted aggressively from the very first moment and controlled.

Poor morale in peacetime will no doubt lead to succumbing to the elements in combat or survival situations. The first essentials in survival situations are the ability to keep your head, to survey the situation coolly, and to take the first step only after dispassionate analytic reasoning. The will to survive is best illustrated in two books: *The Long Walk,* by Slavomir Rawicz, and *The White Rabbit*, by Bruce Marshall.

The Long Walk details Rawicz's life as a Polish Army lieutenant who was imprisoned by the People's Commissariat for Internal Affairs (which was the interior ministry of the Soviet Union) after the German-Soviet invasion of Poland. In a ghostwritten book called *The Long Walk,* he describes that in 1941, he and six others escaped from a Siberian Gulag camp and began a long journey south on foot (about sixty-five hundred kilometers or four thousand miles). They traveled through the Gobi Desert, Tibet, and the Himalayas to finally reach British India in the winter of 1942 (Rawicz, 1956).

The White Rabbit is a nonfiction book based on the experiences of Forest Frederick Edward, a British special operations executive (SOE) agent in the Second World War. Codenamed "SEAHORSE" and "SHELLEY" in the SOE, Yeo-Thomas was known by the Gestapo as the White Rabbit. The British government gave him responsibilities in Occupied and Vichy France because he had lived in France during the interwar years and was fluent in French (Wikipedia, 2020).

An assignment required Yeo-Thomas to parachute into France. Shortly after his arrival, he was betrayed and captured by the Gestapo at the Passy metro station in Paris. The Gestapo took him to their headquarters in Avenue Foch, where he was subjected to brutal torture, including beatings, electric shocks to the genitals, psychological game-playing, sleep deprivation, and repeated submersion in ice-cold water—to the point that artificial respiration was sometimes required (Marshall, 1952).

After the interrogations and torture, he was moved to Fresnes prison. After two failed escape attempts, he was transferred first to Compiegne prison and then to Buchenwald concentration camp. Within these various detention camps, he attempted to organize resistance. Late in the war, he briefly escaped from Buchenwald. On recapture, he was able to pass himself off as a French national and was sent to a "better" camp, where the Nazis sent enlisted Frenchmen, instead of back to Buchenwald. It is reasonable to conclude that his chances of surviving the remainder of the war at Buchenwald were low (Marshall, 1952).

Survival is difficult, but one has only two options if put in a survival situation: give up and die or fight like hell and live.

We stressed to our students the seven enemies of survival and evasion:

1. Pain—Pain can be withstood; one can get used to pain and ignore it, even if it cannot be forgotten.

2. Thirst—If the system lacks liquid, no tablet or other device can replace it. The horrors and dangers of dehydration can only be mitigated by good management of available supplies.

3. Hunger—Unless one eats, one goes hungry. Learn to live off the land, to make what is available last as long as possible, and to go without.

4. Cold—Resistance to cold is almost entirely a question of understanding and practicing survival techniques.

5. Fatigue—Learn the limits of your own endurance, and the onslaught of fatigue will be lessened. Maintain a fitness program and system of regular rest.

6. Boredom and Loneliness—These two are related and, although not as immediately dangerous as the other five, can be fatal to the gregarious individual who has no inward resources to sustain him.

7. Concession to Craving—This aspect of survival only becomes a severe threat when the desire to give in to feelings aroused by the other threats becomes almost unbearable. This dangerous craving must be resisted, and resistance

can only be developed by training. With continued and progressive experience, for example, what was originally an almost overwhelming desire for a drink of water becomes, in time, merely an unpleasant inconvenience.

Section two dealt mainly with the individual's maintenance of their general health, adequate nourishment, the importance of having enough salt and vitamins, sufficient rest, cleanliness, and prevention of infection and disease.

In the military survival situation, the adage "an ounce of prevention is worth a pound of cure" is extremely accurate. In addition to proper nutrition and personal hygiene, every possible preventive measure compatible with the survival situation should be taken to avoid either disease or injury. The phrase "compatible with the survival situation" is necessary because, frequently, the exigencies of survival will require that an injury be incurred and/or neglected temporarily. That is a matter of perspective. Other factors disregarded, even more attention should be devoted to field sanitation and safety than in the typical military situation. In survival, the least incapacity may indicate a chain of events leading to a major disaster due to the lack of outside assistance, including medical care.

Section three was the start of the first-aid sections. In this first section on first-aid, we taught aviators how to provide injury care for critical and life-threatening situations. We included instruction on CPR, different amputation and emergency tracheotomy techniques, how to control bleeding, how to tie off an artery, how to manage pain with the use of painkillers and morphine, and how to treat shock.

Section four addressed the general management of injuries and the proper immobilization of fractures. In this section, we talked about the appropriate immobilization of fractures, and how to minimize infections in the field, clean wounds, change dressings, properly bandage wounds, and use antibiotics. We also provided information about reducing dislocated joints and fractures and how to produce a makeshift cast. We also talked about one of the most critical aspects of the general management of injuries: sterilization of wounds and wound care. A localized infection can spread to become a systemic infection where the whole body is affected. Sepsis occurs when these harmful micro-organisms spread throughout the blood and body tissue. This can lead to multiorgan dysfunction and end up as a limb-or-life-threatening infection.

Burns are frequently encountered in aircraft accidents or during survival episodes, and they pose a severe problem. Burns cause severe pain and predispose a person to shock and infection. Burns also offer an avenue for the considerable loss of body fluids and salts. The initial treatment of a burn is directed toward the relief of pain and the prevention of infection. The closed treatment method has certain advantages over the open treatment advocated in mass casualty situations in the survival situation. Covering the wound with a clean dressing of any type reduces the pain and chances for infection. Furthermore, such protection enhances the patient's mobility and capability to carry out duties and other vital survival functions.

Section five addressed first-aid issues and situations involving a variety of more unique injuries or medical conditions including heat cramps, heat exhaustion, heatstroke, hypothermia, frostbite, trench foot, head wounds, abdomen injuries, chest injuries, eye injuries, thorns and splinters, lacerations, blisters and abrasions, and insect and snake bites.

Section six was specific to survival illnesses. Like injuries, illnesses can take their toll on survivors, and here again, perspective is all-important. Many illnesses that could be considered minor in the standard medical environment can become a significant medical event in the field when a man is on his own and without medical care. Instruction is included on conditions such as food poisoning, respiratory disease, infectious hepatitis, malaria, typhus, skin infections, scabies, and carbon monoxide poisoning.

Section seven provided instruction on escape and evasion and the medical aspects of enemy influence. In escape and evasion, the presence or influence of enemy compounds is important to the application of the survival medicine principles. While the general survival medicine principles and techniques summarized above remain unchanged, their application is made more difficult. In this chapter, the increased risks associated with being captured, mobility, and group versus individual were discussed. These are challenging concepts since we are talking about the difficulties of providing care to a comrade whose treatment may impede the group's evasion efforts due to his condition.

When do you abandon a member of your unit due to incapacitation? In times of war, several unit members' welfare cannot be jeopardized for one's good. Thus, the only option for assuring the escape of the unit's bulk is to abandon an incapacitated member rather than risk the capture of the entire group. This is a difficult decision for most to make, but it is one that, in certain situations, must be made.

Section eight provided instruction on POW compounds and the medical aspects of being an injured POW. Survivors incarcerated within POW enclosures are under the control and mercy of their captors in the physical sense. Thus, the application of survival medicine principles will depend a great deal on the captors' philosophy and the amount of medical service and supplies they can devote to their prisoners. We also discussed these situations and how they applied to the military code of conduct.

Section nine once again focused on survival medicine requirements and the factors impacting those requirements. Throughout the entire manual and training requirements, we stressed military survival, which is defined as returning to friendly control from an emergency anywhere without giving aid or comfort to any enemy.

We also included a snakebite rule, although jungle experts and medics say this method is both outdated and dangerous. Apply a tourniquet between the bite and the heart but only tight enough so that a slight pulse can be felt below the tourniquet. Do not make an incision but suck out the poison from the fang perforations. Sucking by mouth was considered far more effective than any artificial method. If the tourniquet is applied properly, it need not be loosened from time to time. Medics now point out that the incision only increases bleeding and enhances the spread of poison. The bitten area must be kept as cool as possible, and the patient must remain inactive and quiet.

I thought the manual we developed for use at the Navy SERE training school was excellent. We provided the men who attended our training the very best instruction on how to survive in the wilderness and, God forbid, how to survive if they were ever captured by the enemy and became POWs. But as with most things, some did not appreciate our training means and methods.

Finally, we taught the essentials of giving every man who went through our course the opportunity to survive if they found themselves shot down behind enemy lines, injured by a hostile, or taken as a POW. I was confident that the men we were training at SERE school were getting the best instruction possible.

17

COMMANDER JAMES STOCKDALE

ON FEBRUARY 1, 1954, I was promoted to lieutenant commander. It was a proud moment for me. I took tremendous pride in how I handled my responsibilities with the Navy, and SERE training was no different. We were immensely proud of our training, and we believed it gave our people the very best opportunity to survive in the event they were ever captured.

One day, I received a call from Jack Kupsick, one of my E and E class buddies. Jack, who would later go on to become chief of the Operations Division, 6499th Special Activities Group at Hickam Air Force Base, was running the SERE training program at Stead Air Force Base in Reno, Nevada. He asked me to fly up to help entertain and educate several congressmen who were looking into the SERE program. The group wanted a taste of the training and to get a better look at what was going on. We let them stay for three weeks and provided them with a modified version of the training. When they first arrived, they were taken to tents, where they slept. Their bathroom and shower facilities were located outside their tents, a bit inconvenient but a much better situation than those found in most POW camps," which the program was designed to simulate.

After visiting, the congressmen were so impressed with the operation that they appropriated twelve million dollars for the program . . . to spend on a three-story barracks facility to take the place of the tents. They had missed the entire point of SERE training.

I disagreed with the decision to provide "more suitable living conditions" for SERE attendees because one of the training's main points was to learn how to survive in harsh conditions. This was not just a pencil and paper school; it was a hands-on experience designed to simulate being a POW. Our program was a twenty-one-day session intended to train our boys to survive horrible conditions, maintain the will to live, and not crack under tremendous stress and fear. We did not want the training to be more comfortable; we needed the training to be something they had never encountered before and would hopefully never encounter again.

By 1958, the training had been in place for about three years, and I was incredibly pleased and proud of what we were accomplishing. We had set up a SERE training facility at Camp Pendleton, and we were running thirty men through the program each cycle. We were doing great things, so I think you will understand how disappointed I was when I learned that the Navy had been receiving complaints about the difficulties of attending our survival school. It seemed there were a lot of mothers out there who were upset that their sons were going days on end without food and that they were being mistreated by "enemy troops." Well, we were tough, and there were times when the "prisoners" in our camps went without food, but guess what? That was what we were preparing them for, being a POW. We wanted to prepare our people for what they would encounter if, God forbid, they were ever taken captive by an enemy combatant.

Shortly after that call, a Navy commander walked into my office and said, "Lieutenant Commander Conter, I'm commander Jim Stockdale from the Bureau of Personal Naval Aviation in Washington, DC, and I am here because we've had so many complaints from mothers who are writing to their representatives, congressmen, and senators expressing their concerns on how demanding your training is, and they are worried about their sons. They are saying your school is too mean, so the Navy sent me here to check things out, go through the school, and report back to Washington."

I was a bit miffed, but I said fine.

Commander Stockdale requested that he be put through the same training as anyone else attending the SERE training and requested that his identity stay between the two of us. I did not tell anyone who he was. I just told everyone in the training that he was a naval aviator going through the class. We dropped him and his classmates into the northern part of Camp Pendleton and started the attendees' training.

I knew that what we were teaching our students was exactly what they needed to survive being captured by the enemy. It was not an easy training, but if we were going to train a man to prepare himself to be a POW, we had to make the experience as close to real life as possible. I was confident we would get a fair evaluation from Stockdale.

I respected Jim Stockdale. He missed World War II by a few years (he graduated from the Naval Academy in 1947), was assigned as a gunnery officer aboard several ships, and then was accepted for flight training in 1949. He was an aviator, and as such, he knew that he was at risk, as all aviators were, of being shot down and captured by the enemy.

Stockdale was a brilliant guy. Later in his life, he would go on to earn a master's degree in international relations and comparative Marxist thought. In 1962, and according to his biography, he also "tutored a strawberry-haired marine named John Glenn in physics and calculus." For those who do not know, John Glenn would go on to be the first American astronaut to orbit the earth.

Stockdale did the whole program. He did what everyone else in the school did. He had to work his way through the mountains, evade and escape our "enemy" forces, crawl under barbed wire, work his way through mud puddles, and deal with other hazards.

Like all our camp attendees, Stockdale got caught by our enemy soldiers and brought to our POW camp. As a full commander, he was a senior prisoner, and as such, he was interrogated just like the other guys at camp and was not given any special privileges; no one took it easy on him.

Our head interrogator, who was a colonel, knew something was up with Stockdale, came to me, and said, "Lou, that one guy is a plant or something." I played the colonel's comments off by saying, "He is? I didn't know that."

Stockdale completed the course and flew back to Washington, DC, where he reported back to his superiors that while our training was the most challenging and demanding he had ever had, it was also the best training he had ever had and was well worth it.

Some of you already know who Commander Jim Stockdale is. For those of you who do not know his story, a few years after our training, Commander Stockdale went on to be made the commander of an air group aboard the aircraft carrier USS *Oriskany* and was sent to Vietnam. On September 9, 1965, while flying from the USS *Oriskany* on a mission over North Vietnam, Stockdale ejected from his Douglas A-4 Skyhawk, which had been struck by enemy fire and completely disabled. He parachuted into a small village, where he was severely beaten and taken prisoner (Lowry, 1989).

Commander Stockdale was sent to a POW camp in Hoa Lo

Prison—the infamous Hanoi Hilton—where he spent seven and a half years under unimaginably brutal conditions. He was physically tortured no fewer than fifteen times. Techniques included beatings, whippings, and near-asphyxiation with ropes. Mental torture was incessant. He was kept in solitary confinement in total darkness for four years; chained in heavy, abrasive leg irons for two years; malnourished due to a starvation diet; denied medical care; and deprived of letters from home in violation of the Geneva Convention (Stockdale, USN, 2020). It is unimaginable what he must have gone through.

On February 14, 1973, when the first group of twenty former POWs arrived at Travis Air Force Base, California, James Stockdale, who would later become a vice admiral and vice presidential candidate, was the first man to limp off the aircraft. Stockdale paused to thank his countrymen for the loyalty they had shown to him and his fellow POWs: "The men who follow me down that ramp know what loyalty means because they have been living with loyalty, living on loyalty, the past several years—loyalty to each other, loyalty to the military, loyalty to our commander-in-chief" (American Forces Press Service, 2013).

A few days after this historical event, James Stockdale tracked down my phone number and called me. "Lou," he said, "I want to thank you for being so damned tough in that training. Without that training, I would have never lived through my seven and a half years in POW camp."

I must be honest: having Jim Stockdale thank me for what our training did for him and having him express his appreciation for what he was taught in our camp was one of the most rewarding moments of my life. I thought about the representatives, congressmen, senators, and even mothers who were all complaining about how hard we were on our students, and I thought how tragic it would have been if SERE training had been stopped because we were too tough on them. Training our boys right was what was important. Preparing them for the difficulties they would face if they ever became POWs was what was important, and making sure they had the skills to come home if, God forbid, they were ever captured by the enemy was what was important.

Those days—the day Jim Stockdale returned and the days when so many other Vietnam POWS, most of whom had been through our SERE training, came home—were good days. They were days that made me proud to have contributed to ensuring our boys had the best training that they could get and that so many of them had embraced the will to live and had come back to their families and loved ones alive.

18

1953–1967:
THE WONDER YEARS

WHEN I LOOK BACK on my life from 1953 through 1967, I wonder how I ever survived. Even though I was technically in the Naval Reserves, I seemed to be spending more time as a reservist in the military than I was spending as a civilian. I can only describe that time in my life as being the busiest. Even though the Korean War ended in 1953, and even though I was no longer on active duty, my life was a series of military trainings and special assignments, blended with a civilian life that was just as much of a whirlwind.

When I was not on active duty, I called California my home base. I was comfortable there, and it was where my first three kids were living with Katie.

I was so thankful that I had the good sense to keep up on my real estate license. Having the flexibility to be in a profession that allowed me to come and go back and forth into the service was a blessing, and I can't imagine how difficult it would have been to try to hold down any other civilian job and still do all the things that I was doing for the military.

In 1953, I was on one of my extended military stays in

Norfolk, Virginia, when I met Virginia Theresa Bowman at one of the clubs on base, and it did not take long for me to realize I enjoyed being in her company. I was not getting a great deal of free time, but I enjoyed spending time with Virginia when I did.

Virginia was born in Manistee, Michigan, on February 28, 1926, to Harold Bauman and Elizabeth Bauman and was the youngest of five children. When I met Virginia, she was a flight attendant. She was fun to be around, and since she lived in Norfolk, I knew she understood life in the Navy. When I had met Katie, I was in my early twenties and may not have been ready for marriage; now, I was thirty-two (Virginia was twenty-seven). I was older and wiser and ready to settle down again. Virginia and I decided to get married, and we exchanged our vows on January 9, 1954, in Pasquotank, North Carolina.

After we were married, we only stayed on the East Coast for a short time. Now that I was in the civilian world, I was selling real estate, and with California's real estate market booming during the mid-1950s, we knew we needed to live out West.

We hadn't been married long before Virginia was pregnant with our first child, but when she traveled to Pittsburgh, Pennsylvania, for her sister's wedding in July 1954, she was not due for a few months. So imagine my surprise when I received a call that Virginia was having the baby. On July 25, Virginia gave birth to our first child, a daughter, Louann. Like with my first three sons, I was in awe of having another child in my life, but things were a little different this time.

While I love all my boys, there is something special about having a daughter. With all the horrible things I had seen in my life, having Louann helped soften my heart a little. She let me look at things in a different light; she still does.

A few years after Louann was born, we had our second child, a boy, James. Born on April 13, 1957, James was my fifth. A few years later, Jeffery was born on April 9, 1959. We had moved to Walnut Creek, California; I was still serving in the Navy and selling and developing real estate. For a time in the late 1950s, it seemed like I could slow down just a little, enjoy life, and enjoy my children.

Regarding my children, I can tell you this: it did not matter to me what order my kids came into this world; I loved each one of them equally. I consider having children my greatest accomplishment. The fact that all of them turned out to be exceptional people means that the women I married did an excellent job raising them. While I did have a hand in helping raise my children, I have to admit that my wives played a more significant role in making sure the kids stayed on the straight and narrow; I doubt they would have turned out as they did had it not been for their mothers. My military career took me away from home much more than I would have liked, and I was incredibly grateful to both Katie and Virginia for raising such beautiful kids.

In between James and Jeffery, and SERE training schools, I was sent to Rome, Italy, with my old special forces friend Herbie Brucker. We had been deployed on a sensitive mission, but we were enjoying some downtime by having a late dinner and some drinks one night at one of the outside cafés when we suddenly heard a commotion outside another café just a short distance from where we were sitting. A young girl in her early twenties had exited the café, and almost immediately, four big, tough-looking men were moving toward her. Sensing the worst, Herbie and I jumped to our feet and rushed toward the young woman, and the four bruisers headed in her direction. As we approached, Herbie and I quickly developed a plan of how we were going to attack these four monsters, who was taking whom, and how we were going to whisk the woman away to safety. When we were only a few feet away, the woman, clearly recognizing us as Americans, began shouting at us, "No, no, no . . . it's okay; it's okay. They are my bodyguards." The damsel in distress was none other than Sophia Loren. I am extremely confident that Ms. Loren has long forgotten the event, but for Herbie and me, it was a story we have shared with our colleagues and friends over, and over, and over again.

In 1958, I was whisked off to attend the Naval War College in Newport, Rhode Island. The US Naval War College was established in 1884 as an advanced course of professional study for senior naval officers; it educates and develops leaders at specific stages in their careers from all services, US government agencies and departments, and international navies (US Naval War College, 2020).

I enjoyed the teachings at the Naval War College, and they provided a framework for military leaders to gain an understanding of strategy and operations, develop the ability to think critically, learn how to deal with uncertainty and surprise, become proficient in joint matters, comprehend the security environment, and understand all the elements of national power. The course of instruction was tremendous; we had classes in joint military operations, national security decision making, strategy, and policy curriculum, and, of course, the school taught a variety of leadership classes. Every aspect of the US Naval War College was designed to provide attendees with the essential elements of having a successful naval career. It was an amazing experience.

During the late 1950s and early 1960s, Virginia, the kids, and I lived in Whittier, Danville, Walnut Creek, and San Juan Capistrano. I was spending a great deal of time away from home as I was involved in a variety of intelligence operations, setting up SERE training locations all over the world, including Florida, Panama, the Philippines, and Hawaii, and during my time away from my life in the military, I was also working with several different real estate developers, the first of which was the Carl Buck company.

Carl Buck was a well-known builder in Southern California, and he developed dozens of influential residential and commercial projects throughout the region. He had joined his father's building business in the early 1950s, and one of his first significant developments was a large condominium project in Los Angeles. By the late 1950s, Carl was working on some enormous projects. In 1959, the company was involved in a $750-million community development of twenty-five thousand homes and an industrial park that sat on twelve thousand acres in the San Ramon Valley in Alameda and Contra Costa Counties. The proposed development housed 105,000 people (San Francisco Examiner, 1959).

Carl brought me aboard as the vice president of real estate, and I learned a great deal from him. Like me, Carl was an avid golfer and a member of the Bel-Air Country Club, and we even found the time to get in a few rounds occasionally. I enjoyed working with Carl. He was a good guy.

I also spent some time working for Volk-McLain Communities, which was owned and operated by Ken Volk and Robert McLain. Ken was another Navy man who had served during World War II. An Eagle Scout, Ken attended Los Angeles High School and graduated from Stanford University with a bachelor's degree in economics. After the war, Ken formed Volk-McLain Communities, Inc. with Robert (Los Angeles Times, 1996).

In the late 1950s/early 1960s, I became a project coordinator for Volk-McLain Communities, a residential development company. The company had purchased more than four thousand acres of open land in Dublin, California, a small ranching community with a population of less than one thousand.

What made Volk-McLain a dependable development company was that their subdivision used recycled home plans; this means they used the same plans over and over, which allowed them to build homes at a fast pace and with exceptional efficiency. The project in Dublin offered three- and four-bedroom houses. In a short period of time, we had built 234 homes.

Both Ken and Robert were respectable guys, and Ken was

an exceptional businessman; it seemed like every project he touched turned to gold. For example, in 1970, Ken decided to sell his share of Volk-McLain. A few months later, he partnered up with a gentleman named Wayne Hughes. Hughes was looking for an investor to form a new business, and Ken was looking for a unique investment opportunity. It was a gamble, to be sure, and not many people would put much faith in Wayne's idea that people needed a self-storage unit away from their homes. Ken decided to roll the dice with Wayne; the men ponied up twenty-five thousand dollars each and formed a company called Public Storage, which is "the largest owner of self-storage facilities in the United States and has more than 2400 locations throughout North America and Europe" (Commercial Real Estate, 2019). Ken's twenty-five-thousand-dollar investment probably made him more money than his real estate development deals.

One of the more significant developments I was involved with was a community in Alamo, California. The community was built in conjunction with the Round Hill County Club. The club was beautiful, and I was fortunate to have played many rounds of golf there.

Development and construction seemed to be where my interests had taken me. It was a business I excelled at, and it helped me provide for my family. Throughout the late '50s and early '60s, I worked for a variety of companies in various roles. I was a sales manager for both the Devon Construction Company and the La Mirada Development Company, and I served as the vice president of the Westfield Development Company for a while.

In the early 1960s, as happy as I was and as busy as I was, I got the brilliant idea I wanted to own a ranch. I found a fantastic piece of property in Imlay, Nevada, between Lovelock and Winnemucca. I obtained a little more than thirty-five thousand deeded acres, and I leased another 1.2 million acres from the

Bureau of Land Management (BLM). I named the property the Big Dipper Ranch, and I could not tell you why we chose that name, but we did. We had nearly 1,250 head of cattle and twenty-two hundred head of sheep.

I will be honest; my primary interest in the property was to have it as a real estate investment. It was a steal of a deal, and I knew that if we held on to the property for a few years, it would turn a pretty good profit. I also thought that I would enjoy owning a ranch and being a rancher, but quite frankly, it was one of the most miserable experiences of my life. Heck, I did not even enjoy riding a horse.

I had five men who worked at a time at the camp. They did all the typical ranch duties such as taking care of the day-to-day needs of the animals. The men ensured the herd got to a good grazing area and were provided healthcare; basically, they tended to every need they had, which could become significant and expensive.

Due to the lease with BLM, the wild horses were rounded up and given shots every six months to keep the herd healthy. The sick ones were sold off to packing houses. The rest were sent back out to run until the next roundup. It was hard work, to be sure, but the cowboys we had were hard workers; they worked thirty days straight and there were times where they put in sixteen-hour days.

The cowboys were a bit of a handful as well. After working thirty days, each cowboy was given ten days off. The areas had several brothels, so when they got paid, they went to the brothels and bars and spent all their money. The girls used to know when it was payday and would drive up to the ranch and stay at the camp for three or four days. I did not know what was going on for the longest time, but when I found out about it, I put an end to it. Back in the 1960s, the bunkhouse was no place for a

woman, so I had to stop the "social sleepovers." We started paying the cowboys once a month—right after their thirtieth day of
work and right before the start of their ten-day-off period. The
guys took their money and went on their way.

· I can't tell you how many times my ranch manager and I had
to go into town and pick up one of our cowboys, who may have
either been a bit too rambunctious or had run out of money, but
I will give them credit: they were a surly group, but if you are
going to be a cowboy, that's pretty much how you have to be in
order to be good at what you do.

I had no idea how hard ranching was. Not that I minded
hard work, but at the time, I was still setting up SERE programs
and being placed on active duty every once in a while for a special operation. I did not have the time to be a full-time rancher,
and if you know anything at all about ranching, you know it's a
profession that requires your attention twenty-four hours a day,
seven days a week, 365 days a year.

Ultimately, I found out that it was awful trying to run that
ranch. It was too much of a job. The primary reason I had bought
the place was that it was a steal, but after I learned how hard
running that place was, I had to get out of the ranching business.

We probably had the ranch for two years, which was long
enough to say that I was a big-time rancher for a while. When
we sold the property, we ended up making money on the trans-
action. A short while ago, I saw that the ranch had been listed in
a rancher magazine for twelve million dollars.

After we sold the ranch, my family and I returned to city life.
Then, as life would have it, the military came calling once again,
and I was placed on active duty.

As I said earlier, many of the "old-timers" who were in special forces and involved in conducting various clandestine operations would never think of sharing with the world the details of

the missions we were engaged in executing. We were sworn to se-
crecy for life—not five years, not until we got out of the service.
I think it is wrong for military people to get out of the military
and write a book about their secret missions. Talking about your
military experiences is one thing; talking about secret missions
is a completely different deal.

Top secret for life means just that: top secret for life. Did I
engage in several missions that fall into the "secret for life" cate-
gory? Yes, I did. And, yes, there were times when these missions
called me away from my roles and responsibilities in the civilian
world, and, yes, there were times when I was called away from
my family to engage in these clandestine operations, but I was
proud to do what was asked of me in service to our country, and
you will never hear me speak of these missions, nor will you
see anything considered top secret written in this book, even if
those missions have since been declassified.

In 1962, I was on a special task force recommending that the
Defense Intelligence Agency be set up to coordinate all intelligence of the Navy, Army, Air Force, and Marines along with the
CIA. It was also about this time that President John F. Kennedy
was being pulled in different directions regarding America's involvement in Vietnam.

John Fitzgerald Kennedy was a fervent believer in contain-
ing communism. In his first speech upon becoming president,
Kennedy made it clear that he would continue the policy of the
former president, Dwight Eisenhower, and support the government of Diem in South Vietnam. Kennedy also made it plain
that he supported the domino theory, and he was convinced that
if South Vietnam fell to communism, then other states in the
region would, too, as a consequence. Kennedy was not prepared
to contemplate this (Trueman, 2015).

However, Kennedy received conflicting advice with regard to

Vietnam. Charles De Gaulle warned him that warfare in Vietnam would trap America in a "bottomless military and political swamp." This was based on France's experience at Dien Bien Phu, which left a sizable psychological scar on French foreign policy for some years. However, Kennedy had more daily contact with hawks in Washington, DC, who believed that American forces would be far better equipped and prepared for conflict in Vietnam than the French had been. They believed that even a small increase in US support for Diem would ensure success in Vietnam. The hawks, in particular, were strong supporters of the domino theory (Trueman, 2015).

In 1963, I was part of a five-man team that went to Vietnam and conducted a full assessment of what was taking place in the country. By that time, we had about twelve hundred intelligence and special forces men behind the lines in North Vietnam, and we had about sixteen thousand US "military advisers" in South Vietnam.

After we completed our assessment, our group met with President Kennedy, and we advised him that an escalation of the war was not in the best interest of our country. When I left that meeting, I believed that President Kennedy would not push more troops into Vietnam and that he would be pulling our advisers out of the county. Tragically, a few weeks after our meeting with him, President Kennedy was assassinated.

When people ask me who I think killed President Kennedy, I always tell them that a general rule of thumb in any assassination of a head of state is simple: find out who benefits the most by that person's death, and that person or group will be your primary suspect(s). Who assumes that person's power and who benefits financially from that person's death is usually key to finding who is behind any murder.

I do not want to put forth a conspiracy theory on President Kennedy's assassination, nor do I want to provide a history lesson on the Vietnam War. However, there is no doubt that when President Kennedy was murdered, Vice President Lyndon Johnson became the most powerful man in the world. Within a day or two of Kennedy's murder, President Johnson told the members of the advisement team committee that he "would make up his own mind about how to handle Vietnam." On November 26, 1963, just four days after President Kennedy was assassinated, President Johnson approved NSAM 273, a national security agency memorandum that directed the US government "to assist the people and Government of South Vietnam to win their contest against the externally directed and supported Communist conspiracy."

The war killed 58,220 American soldiers and wounded 153,303 more (Rohn, 2014). Another 1,643 were missing in action. North Vietnam lost 1.1 million soldiers, while 250,000 South Vietnamese soldiers died. Both sides lost more than two million civilians (Vietnam Embassy in Pyongyang, 2019).

Vietnam was the most heavily bombed country in history. More than 6.1 million tons of bombs were dropped, compared to 2.1 million tons in World War II (Clearwater County Veterans Memorial, 2020). The United States spent $843.63 billion (in 2019 dollars) from 1965 to 1973 (Harrington & Suneson, 2019), and several people and companies made a great deal of money as a result of our going to war in Vietnam.

I have strong doubts about the theory that was put forth by the Warren Commission that Lee Harvey Oswald was a malcontent lone wolf. According to the commission, President Kennedy was assassinated by Lee Harvey Oswald, and Oswald acted alone. As someone who had been training potential POWs, after his capture by his enemies, Oswald knew precisely what to do and what to say. The way he handled himself in captivity proved to me, and many others in the intelligence community, that he was well schooled on how to carry himself if he were captured.

Oswald's effective interrogation and his involvement in President Kennedy's assassination became a moot point when Jack Ruby silenced him, killing Oswald on November 24, 1963.

I also have strong doubts that Jack Ruby acted alone when he killed Oswald two days after the Kennedy assassination. Jack may have been the trigger man, but I have reservations about the concept that he hatched the idea of killing Oswald all by himself.

Several members in the intelligence community saw proof that Lee Harvey Oswald was at Lyndon Johnson's ranch in Texas just three days before Kennedy's assassination. Why would this be? How could this be? That is probably a story for another book.

So who do I believe was responsible for killing President Kennedy? Again, I go back to the fundamental questions of who assumed his position of power and who benefited from his death.

I liked John F. Kennedy. He was going to pull our boys out of Vietnam, and I believed he would do good things for our country. I did not particularly care for Lyndon Johnson. He was a man of tremendous legislative skills but was not a particularly good people person.

By the early to mid-1960s, it seemed as if I was getting pulled in more and more directions by the Navy. I was also trying to juggle work and have some semblance of a home life; it was a challenge. My time away from home had been taking its toll on Virginia. I was away a great deal, and when I was home, I was busy working real estate and land development projects. We were arguing more and more, and she was growing more resentful of all the time I was spending with my Navy responsibilities, which was understandable.

Looking back on things, I think the beginning of the end of my marriage with Virginia came when the Navy gave me orders to report to Hawaii and put together another SERE school. I probably could have called it a career at this point in my life, but I knew the war in Vietnam was going to escalate in a big way, and I also knew the SERE trainings we were doing were important. I felt an obligation to continue to serve my country for as long as I could, so I packed up once again, left my family, and reported for duty.

19

MY FIRST TRIP TO THE
USS *ARIZONA* MEMORIAL

AS I AM SURE you can understand, Hawaii was full of bitter-
sweet memories for me. While I had some beautiful memories
of Hester and her family, at the same time, just as thousands of
other military and civilians who were in Hawaii during the Japanese attack on Oahu, the island left me with some pretty horrific
memories as well.

As I shared earlier, when I returned to Hawaii in the 1950s
and had taken a trip to the USS *Arizona*, the only structure hon-
oring my fallen shipmates was a wooden platform. By the mid-
1960s, however, the memorial was the structure you see today.

The history of the USS *Arizona* memorial is a fascinating
tale. In 1949, the Pacific War Memorial Commission was created to build a permanent memorial in Hawaii. A year later, Admiral Arthur W. Radford, commander of the Pacific Fleet, attached
a flag pole to the USS *Arizona's* main mast in 1950 and began a
tradition of hoisting and lowering the flag. Progress on the memorial moved along slowly until 1958, when President Dwight
D. Eisenhower approved the creation of a national memorial and
enabled legislation that called for it to be budgeted at $500,000

and privately financed (even though $220,000 was government subsidized). Other contributors to the memorial came from the following: The Territory of Hawaii (initial contribution in 1958) gave fifty thousand dollars; Ralph Edwards raised more than ninety-five thousand dollars following the 1958 showing of his television series, *This Is Your Life*. The segment featured Rear Admiral (ret.) Samuel G. Fuqua, Medal of Honor recipient and the senior surviving officer from the USS *Arizona*. Elvis Presley did a benefit concert on March 25, 1961, at Bloch Arena in Hawaii and raised sixty-four thousand dollars. Hawaii Senator Daniel Inouye initiated legislation from federal funds, and in a partnership between the Fleet Reserve Association and Revell Model Company, forty thousand dollars was raised from the sale of plastic models of the USS *Arizona* (Arizona Memorial Museum Association, 2005). The memorial was formally dedicated on May 30, 1962.

A few weeks after I arrived in Hawaii, Roy L. Johnson, admiral of the Pacific Fleet, who was stationed in Hawaii, sent word that I was to meet him at the dock leading to the USS *Arizona* at 1300 hours. Needless to say, when you get word that a four-star admiral has ordered you to be somewhere at a specific time, you do it with no questions asked.

I admired Admiral Johnson. As a junior officer, he served aboard the USS *Tennessee*, a battleship. His next assignment was to serve on Commander Battleship Divisions' staff, Battle Fleet, under Admiral Frank H. Schofield. After his duty on the battleships, he went to flight school, earned his wings, and became a naval aviator who served with Patrol Squadron Twelve (he was a PBY pilot). In early WWII, he served in various administrative jobs before being transferred to Fleet Air Command, Naval Air Station Quonset Point, as commander Carrier Air Group Two in May 1943. In early 1944, the air group joined the aircraft carrier USS *Hornet* (CV-12). As air group commander (CAG), he directed and led attacks against Japanese forces at Palau, Woleai, Wake Island, and Truk, striking enemy aircraft, airfields, shipping, and shore installations. For his CAG service, he was awarded the Air Medal. Later, he received the Bronze Star Medal and a second Legion of Merit, with Combat "V" for his service in action, which included campaigns against Japanese forces in the Philippines, Iwo Jima, and Okinawa. He also wore a Presidential Unit Citation, which was awarded to the USS *Hornet* for her part in these campaigns (San Francisco Chronicle, 1999). His post-World War II military career was equally impressive, and I would encourage anyone reading this book to research Admiral Johnson to learn more about this incredible man. His life and military career will amaze you.

Admiral Johnson had just received his fourth star and had been named the commander in chief, US Pacific Fleet. While in this capacity, he had over 450 vessels under his command and had Fleet Marine Force, Pacific, under his operational control. Under his command, the units conducted airstrikes against North Vietnam's targets, including the enemy's supply installations.

I met the admiral at 1300 hours as I was instructed to do, and he had four or five people with him. He told me we were going to visit the memorial. I replied, "Yes, sir," and we boarded the admiral's barge and headed toward the USS *Arizona*. I must admit that when I saw the memorial, I had a bit of anxiety; there were so many memories. As we were getting closer, all I could do was watch it come closer and closer.

We tied up to the dock, and Admiral Johnson said, "Conter, go aboard." I disembarked the barge and stepped onto a small docking platform, faced aft, saluted, and then made my way toward the entry to the memorial.

Back in the 1960s, the memorial's entrance was not like it is today; then, once you left the dock, you would ascend a group of stairs that led to the entry room. From the entry room, which is the first of three main rooms of the USS *Arizona* Memorial, I entered the second room or the assembly hall, as it is known. This part of the memorial has seven large windows on both walls at the end of the room that goes up and opens to the ceiling. The seven windows refer to the date of the attack, December 7, and throughout the assembly hall, there are twenty-one windows, which represent an ever-present twenty-one-gun salute. There is a hole cut in the floor so that visitors can look down at the wreckage still submerged in the oil-slicked waters. As I progressed toward the shrine room and the memorial wall, I kept saying to myself that I had to remain strong.

Entering the shrine room was pretty rough. Seeing the names of 1,177 of my shipmates on the wall nearly took my breath away and knocked me out. I cannot tell you how long I stood before the wall staring at the names. I continued to say to myself, *You must be strong. You must be strong. You must be strong.*

I remember saying a prayer—a long prayer. I remember saluting, and I remember thinking that I needed to be a military man about things, but it was awfully hard to stand in the shrine room before the names of my shipmates and friends who were lost that day.

I saw Curtis Haynes's name on the wall. If you remember, Curtis was the quartermaster second class who was ordered by Captain Van Valkenberg to follow him to the bridge on December 7, 1941. I reflected for a moment about how easily my name could have been on that wall and wondered why it was not.

I probably spent about forty to forty-five minutes on the memorial. I am not sure why the admiral reached out to me and ordered me to accompany him there, but I am grateful he did. It was extremely hard to do, but after giving it some thought on the return trip back to the dock, I realized I needed to make that visit, and I was glad that I did it.

Most of us who survived the attack on the USS *Arizona* and Pearl Harbor knew how fortunate we were to have lived through the Japanese attack. I was no different, and I thank God every day for all the blessings in my life: my family, my friends, my health. I was one of the lucky ones who went on to live my life, do some fantastic things, and meet some incredible people. Life could have ended for me on December 7, 1941, just as it did for 1,177 of my friends and shipmates.

By the mid-1960s, we had SERE training all throughout the United States and in some other countries. Naval Air Station Brunswick in Maine offered a twelve-day code of conduct course designed to give Navy pilots and aircrew the skills necessary to survive and evade capture and, if captured, resist interrogation and escape. A second school was opened so that other US Navy and Marine Corps troops, such as sea, air, and land (SEAL) teams, special warfare combatant-craft crewmen, explosive ordnance disposal, Marine RECON (reconnaissance units), US Marine special operations units, and Navy combat medics could attend. The Pickel Meadow camp, where Marines were being trained in outdoor survival in the 1950s and which became known as the Mountain Warfare Training Center (MCMWTC), was up and running in Bridgeport, California, along with Jungle Operations Training Centers at Fort Sherman in Panama (also known as Green Hell), Camp Gonsalves in northern Okinawa, Japan, and Clark Air Base in the Philippines.

I felt good about the SERE training program we developed in Hawaii; more importantly, I felt confident that the men being sent into Vietnam had the tools to come home safely, if, God forbid, they were ever captured by the enemy. Once everything was in place, I left Hawaii and joined my family in Danville, California.

When I returned home, things between Virginia and me were noticeably different. We were different people from when we were first married. Like with my first marriage, I think the primary reason for the marriage having failed was due to the circumstances of my military career. Looking back on my first two marriages, I can see why things just did not work out.

The strains that my constant deployments must have created on Katie and Virginia had to be difficult on them. It probably did not help much that the jobs I was doing at the time were classified, which meant when I was away, I couldn't talk to them about what I was doing, and when I returned, I couldn't talk to them about what I had done. Even now, deployed members of the military have higher-than-average divorce rates compared to the general civilian population. The Air Force is the highest at 14.6 percent, the Navy is at 12.5 percent, and the Marines and Army are both over 8 percent.

In November of 1966, Virginia and I were divorced. Unlike my divorce from Katie, I knew the reasons Virginia and I ended our marriage. Again, just like my marriage to Katie, there were so many things about my marriage to Virginia that were right, and the only things that prevented us from having a long and successful marriage were my military commitments—the jobs I was assigned to and all the time I spent away from home, both when I was on active military duty and when I was selling and developing property. I was a workaholic—I knew it, and so did Virginia.

I had been in the service since 1939. I had given twenty-eight years of my life to the service of my country, and I more than likely had sacrificed two marriages because of my service to my country. Since I had not completed college, I was not going to promote any higher in rank; I was stuck at being a lieutenant commander. So in December of 1967, it was time to call it a career and move on to the next chapter in my life.

I am often asked what I think went right and what I think went wrong in my first two marriages, and my response is always the same: everything but my serving in the military was right about my first two marriages. I had three exceptional children with each of my wives, all of whom I am immensely proud of every day. However, I believe that the demands of my military career eventually took their toll on those relationships. I will say that I do not have any regrets about either of my marriages, nor do I have any regrets about serving in the military. These were two elements of my life that just never seemed to get along very well.

20

I'M OFF TO CAMELOT

WITHIN A FEW WEEKS of leaving the Navy, I got a call from Edward L. Johnson, president of the Financial Federation. He asked, "What are you doing, Lou?" When I told him I had just left the service, he said, "Well, good. You're now the vice president of real estate at Coachella Valley Savings and Loan." I said, "Where's that?" He said, "Palm Springs," so I got in my car and drove to Palm Springs.

I walked in and announced who I was and that I was the new vice president of real estate. Then I asked, "What do we have here?" Well, what I learned was we had a mess—a big one.

"Financial Federation lost $8.6 million in 1966, stemming from a $10.4 million allocation to reserves against possible losses on the sale of foreclosed properties and investments. In the first three months of this year (1967), a $1.18 million loss was reported" (Sederberg, 1967). I was brought in to help fix things.

My first task was to clean up some of the Financial Federation's property issues. The group owned 310 lots, thirty-five houses, and a little more than two million dollars of real-estate-owned property, which is property owned by a lender, such as a bank, that has not been successfully sold at a foreclosure auction. My job was to get rid of the property.

The price of the homes held by the Financial Federation had been forty-six thousand dollars, and they were not moving, so I lowered the price to $35,500, and within thirty days, every single home sold. Yes, the prices were cut, but Financial Federation was still making a profit—and a pretty good one at that.

One day, a woman named Lindsay Deverich came in to look at one of the model homes. She had three children with her, one of them being Laura, whom I recognized as a classmate and friend of my daughter, Louann. Lindsay had taken a liking to one of the four-bedroom, three-bath houses that we still had in our inventory, so I told her I could sell it to her for $35,500.

She agreed, and when I asked if she needed a loan for the mortgage, she said, "No, my friend Jack Warner is taking care of the financing for me." For those of you who may not know the name Jack Warner, he and three of his brothers founded Warner Brothers movie studios in 1923, and the studio is still considered one of the Big Five major American film studios.

She told me she would have someone from Jack's office call, and sure enough, the next day, I got a call from Jack's right-hand man, who asked if I could meet Jack that coming Friday at a restaurant on Sunset Boulevard. I do not remember which restaurant it was, but when I arrived, Jack was there waiting. We exchanged pleasantries, had a few drinks, and had dinner. After a couple of hours, we decided to call it a night. Then Jack handed me an envelope. "This is for the house," he said. "Don't worry; it's all there."

I took the envelope from Jack and immediately put it in my jacket pocket without looking inside. We shook hands and went our separate ways. When I got to my car, I opened the envelope and saw one-hundred-dollar bills—a lot of them. In fact, there was thirty-five thousand dollars in one-hundred-dollar bills.

It took me a moment to realize that I had a great deal of cash on me, and to be frank, I was not at all comfortable having that much money on my person, so I decided to return to my office in Palm Springs and locked it in my desk. On Monday morning, I put the funds into an escrow account for Lindsay, and a short while later, she moved into the development.

I must admit I was a bit surprised to learn that Jack Warner was such a down-to-earth person. Sure, it was only one dinner, but Jack came across as just a regular guy. He was very personable, not at all snobbish, and not at all full of himself, as many movie moguls are rumored to be. I did not talk about my experience aboard the USS *Arizona*, but I found it a bit ironic that my path would cross with Jack Warner, if for no other reason than Warner Brothers had produced a film in 1934 called *Here Comes the Navy*, which was a romantic comedy filmed aboard the USS *Arizona*.

A few weeks after my dinner with Jack, Lindsay called and asked me if I had a tuxedo. I said, "Yes, I have a tux. Why?" Her response was that Warner Brothers was having a movie premiere for the film *Camelot* in Palm Springs, and her daughter, Laura, wanted Louann to come to the dinner and the premiere of the film, which starred Richard Harris as King Arthur, Vanessa Redgrave as Guinevere, and Franco Nero as Lancelot.

I believe the film really had three premieres: one in New York, another in London, and the third in Palm Springs at the Camelot Theatre, located near the Palm Springs Mall. It was a 625-seat theater that opened on February 4, 1967, at a cost of $750,000, so it was a fancy place, a complete state-of-the-art theater, and a fantastic location to hold a premiere.

I broke out my tuxedo, got Louann a new dress, and we went to our first movie premiere. Never having been to a Hollywood event like this, I was not sure what to expect. When we arrived at the dinner, Louann and I were escorted to our table, where we were seated with Laura and her aunt, Valerie (Lindsay's sister). Throughout the course of the evening, I found Val to be an exceptionally wonderful person. She was witty, engaging, and an overall lovely lady.

We enjoyed a tremendous evening together. I would later learn that Lindsay and the girls, Louann and Laura, had set the whole thing up, and I was delighted that they did. Since it had not been long since my divorce, I was not ready to jump back into the dating scene right away, so I waited a week before I called Val and asked her out to dinner. It was clear from the start that she was a special lady.

When Val and her husband divorced, she and her son Ron, who I believe was eighteen at the time, had moved with Lindsay into the house that Jack had purchased. Val worked at one of the local hospitals in the emergency room's office area, and I was working hard selling houses, but we still found time to catch lunch or dinner together. There were even a few nights when we managed to take in a movie.

We enjoyed each other's company, and neither one of us was looking to rush into a serious relationship, but after about two months, Val told me she did not want to date anyone else. I did not have a problem with that, and I felt the same way toward her, so I guess that was when we officially became a couple.

At the end of the school year, the kids moved back to Danville with Virginia, and toward the end of the year, Coachella Savings and Loan had nine thousand acres outside of Lodi that they wanted me to develop and sell, so I was going to have to relocate again. By this time, Val and I were serious about one another, so she decided to move with me. It took us about eight months to complete the job, and then we returned to Southern California for a brief time. On July 9, 1969, Val and I were married at a small chapel in Van Nuys, California; Lindsay was the only one at the ceremony.

In 1969, Val and I were off to Bend, Oregon, where, once

again, there were lots that needed to be developed into single-family homes. It took us about three years to develop 435 properties. We were busy, but Val and I enjoyed our time in Bend; it was a beautiful part of the country.

In 1972, I was approached by Westfield Development to build out a subdivision in National City, which is near San Diego. Val and I moved to San Juan Capistrano, and I must admit we both enjoyed living in that community. In addition to being the home of the miracle of the swallows (which takes place each year at Mission San Juan Capistrano when the swallows migrate six thousand miles from Goya, Argentina, to San Juan Capistrano), the city is the site of California's oldest residential neighborhood, Los Rios. San Juan Capistrano is also the home of the oldest in-use building in California, the Serra Chapel in the Mission. In addition, the city is the home of both the first vineyard and the first winery in California. We stayed in San Juan Capistrano until 1981. Then we moved to Indian Wells, located near Palm Springs.

I was sixty years old. I was too young to start thinking about retiring, but I had been pushing myself so hard for so long that it was time to take a break, not work as hard, spend some quality time with Val, and start playing a little more golf. We purchased a nice home on the seventh fairway of the Indian Wells Country Club.

Val started working at the hospital, and I joined the Indian Wells Country Club and started golfing. I was still doing some real estate things, but one of the lessons I learned early in my life from my first father-in-law, Ed Loftus, was that golf courses are where people with money frequent, and many business deals are made on the golf course. So even though I was not working, in a way I was.

I enjoy golfing, and up until a few years ago, I tried to play as much as I could. It is a great way to get exercise, relax, meet a few new business contacts, and maybe make a few business transactions.

In 1981, I decided to play in the Bob Hope Desert Classic (which was later renamed the Bob Hope Chrysler Classic in 1986). The event had five rounds of competition for professionals and four rounds for amateurs and was known for its celebrity Pro-Am rounds, which teamed up three amateur golfers with a professional. The event brought in some of Hollywood's biggest stars of the time such as Frank Sinatra, Jack Benny, Sammy Davis, Jr., Dean Martin, Joey Bishop, Burt Lancaster, Kirk Douglas, Phil Harris, Ray Bolger, Hoagy Carmichael, Desi Arnaz (who was one of the founders of my club, Indian Wells), and several professional athletes; even Dwight Eisenhower (the first US president to play in the Pro-Am) and President Gerald R. Ford played in the tournament.

The cost of playing in the tournament was ten thousand dollars, but since Indian Wells was one of the tournament's courses, the cost for members was thirty-five hundred dollars. I played in six of the tournaments: 1981, 1983, 1984, 1985, 1993, and 1996.

I was a ten handicap golfer, which is not too bad for an amateur, and had the chance to play with Jay Haas, who has eighteen Professional Golf Association (PGA) wins; Dave Stockton, who has ten PGA wins; Cory Paven, who has fifteen PGA wins and with whom our team won the tournament; Lee Travino, who has twenty PGA wins; and Arnold Palmer, who has sixty-two PGA wins. The year I was on Arnold Palmer's team, we sure had a great time, even though we did not win the tournament. Palmer was a really nice guy, a true gentleman, and a class act. One year, I was on a team with singer Johnny Mathis. Mathis was a tremendous golfer, and in fact, he was an outstanding athlete. In high school, he was a basketball and track star, and in college—I believe he went to San Francisco State College—he set the high-jump record and was an Olympic-level athlete. What a great guy!

By that time, Val had taken up golf. She had met a few gals at the club, and while she did not ever play in the tournament, she did become a Bob Hope Girl, a role she held for twenty years. Val was assigned to the third hole, which was featured the closest to the hole competition. She had a ball being a part of the tournament.

One of the best parts of being involved in the Bob Hope Pro-Am was that the people involved in the event, from the organizers to the workers and celebrities, were all quality folks. After the round was done, everyone would go to the clubhouse for drinks and conversation. One of the best clubhouse comedians was Joey Bishop. He was extremely funny, except when he tried to hit on Val. All joking aside, everyone involved was just fantastic.

We also met some good contacts along the way, one of whom was Bing Crosby. Bing and I got to talking, and I learned that he had a house for sale in Coeur d'Alene, Idaho, so I bought it. He even threw in some furniture! I also purchased a grape vineyard in Modesto from Crosby. Like Bob Hope, Bing was a strong supporter of our military. He was not as visible as Bob, but he was a strong supporter nonetheless.

As for Bob Hope, he was nothing but a class act. I always appreciated everything Bob did for the military's men and women, and at the golf tournament, he was the same person you saw on television. He was very personable, he treated everyone exceptionally well, and he was just a good guy. Oh, yes, and Bob Hope was funny. One day, Val took me to a men's clothing store in Palm Springs—she wanted me to buy a pair of pink pants—and I told her, "Men do not wear pink pants." All of a sudden, we heard a familiar voice yell from across the store, "Val, buy him the pink pants; he would look good in them." It was Bob Hope.

We ended up chatting in the store for a while, and then we bought the pink pants. I still have them today. I wear them once a year for breast cancer awareness day; I also wear a pink shirt and pink socks—the whole nine yards.

I must say that it was fun taking one day a year to hobnob with the rich and famous. One of the lessons I learned from my experience with the Bob Hope Classic was that Hollywood had some good people and that most of the stars were regular guys who ended up making some good friends. It was a great time. The Bob Hope Desert Classic was good to us; thanks for the memories, Mr. Hope.

21

OUR FIRST REMEMBRANCE
CEREMONY

IN 1991, VAL AND I made a big decision; we were going to
go to the Pearl Harbor Remembrance Ceremony. I'm not sure
how word got out that I was an USS *Arizona* survivor, but a few
months before the fiftieth anniversary on the attack on Pearl
Harbor, I received a call from a history teacher in Palm Desert
who had known about my history and that I was involved in
the local Pearl Harbor Survivors Chapter. He asked if I could get
some of the survivors together and come to the school to give a
briefing on Pearl Harbor and World War II. There were four or
five of us who went to give a fifty-minute presentation. Some of
the other teachers dropped in on the class, and as soon as one
period ended, another teacher would ask us to come and talk to
their class. We ended up spending the entire day there. It was
great.

In the years that followed, we began giving presentations to
the five high schools in the district. We did not do it class by
class but talked at a school assembly and usually spoke before
twelve hundred to fifteen hundred students. We had about four
or five guys who would talk for ten to fifteen minutes each, and

then we would take questions from the kids. I helped organize those talks until Val and I left for Oregon in 1996.

Since then, I have talked to a wide variety of groups and organizations everywhere we have lived, and not only do I consider it my responsibility to do so, but I consider it a tremendous honor.

The Fiftieth Anniversary and Remembrance Ceremony was a big deal, and there was a full slate of events for the survivors and their families. There were floral offerings, flyovers, ships salutes, and military band concerts. There were reunions of various groups associated with the attack on Pearl Harbor, flag raising ceremonies, parades, and memorial services.

In 1991, only thirty-one USS *Arizona* survivors attended the ceremony; I don't know how many survivors were remaining, but there were only 335 of us who survived the attack, so I don't imagine there were too many more than the thirty-one who were in attendance.

Guest speakers at the remembrance ceremony included Honolulu Mayor Frank Fasi, Hawaii Governor John Waihee, Hawaii Senator Daniel Inouye, and the keynote speaker was President George H. W. Bush.

Like me, President Bush was a naval aviator. He, too, was shot down during World War II:

> With the wings of his plane on fire and smoke pouring into the cockpit, future President George H. W. Bush parachuted into the Pacific Ocean, where he floated for hours on a life raft, vomiting uncontrollably and bleeding profusely from his forehead. Still, Bush could count himself among the lucky ones. Rescued from the water by a U.S. submarine, he managed to avoid the grisly fate suffered by so many airmen during World War II, including his two crewmates, who both died in the attack.

Soldiers who fought in World War II, the deadliest conflict in history, performed any number of risky jobs. Of
these, few, if any, were as perilous as flying in an airplane
(Greenspan, 2019).

I respected George H. Bush as a naval aviator and as our
president, and he delivered a powerful and emotional speech on
December 7, 1941, and even shed a few tears. His speech had
nothing to do with politics that day. It was an American talking
about other Americans and the bravery they displayed under
horrible circumstances. I like what the president said that day. It
touched my heart.

The following remarks were delivered by President Bush to
World War II veterans and families at Kilo 8 Pier, Honolulu,
Hawaii, on December 7, 1991—the fiftieth anniversary of Pearl
Harbor Day:

I expect if we went around the room, all of us would remember. I remember exactly when I first heard the news
about Pearl Harbor. I was 17 years old, walking across the
green at school. And my thoughts in those days did not
run to world events, but mainly to simpler things, more
mundane things like making the basketball team or entering college. And that walk across the campus marked
an end of innocence for me.

When Americans heard the news, they froze in shock.
But just as quickly we came together. Like all American
kids back then, I was swept up in it. I decided that very
day to go into the Navy to become a Navy pilot. And so,
on my 18th birthday—June 12, 1942—I was sworn into
the Navy as a Seaman Second Class.

And I was shocked—I was shocked at my first sight of
Pearl Harbor several months later—April of '44. We came

into port on the carrier *San Jacinto*. Nearby, the *Utah* was still on her side, parts of the USS *Arizona* still stood silent in the water. Everywhere the skeletons of ships reached out as if to demand remembrance and warn us of our own mortality.

Over 2,000 men died in a matter of minutes on this site, a half century ago. Many more died that same day as Japanese forces assaulted the Philippines and Guam and Wake Island, Midway, Malaya, Thailand, Singapore, Hong Kong. On that day of infamy, Pearl Harbor propelled each of us into a titanic contest for mankind's future. It galvanized the American spirit as never before into a single-minded resolve that could produce only one thing—victory . . .

We triumphed, despite the fact that the American people did not want to be drawn into the conflict—"the unsought war," it's been called. Ironically, isolationists gathered together at what was known in those days as an "America First" rally in Pittsburgh—at precisely the moment the first Americans met early, violent deaths right here at Pearl Harbor. The isolationists failed to see that the seeds of Pearl Harbor were sown back in 1919, when a victorious America decided that in the absence of a threatening enemy abroad, we should turn all of our energies inward. That notion flew escort for the very bombers that attacked our men 50 years ago . . .

In remembering, it is important to come to grips with the past. No nation can fully understand itself or find its place in the world if it does not look with clear eyes at all the glories and disgraces, too, of the past. We in the United States acknowledge such an injustice in our own history: The internment of Americans of Japanese ancestry was a great injustice, and it will never be repeated.

The values we hold dear as a nation—equality of opportunity, freedom of religion and speech and assembly, free and vigorous elections—are now revered by many nations. Our greatest victory in World War II took place not on the field of battle, but in nations we once counted as foes. The ideals of democracy and liberty have triumphed in a world once threatened with conquest by tyranny and despotism . . .

Recently, a letter arrived from the son of a Pearl Harbor survivor, a Navy man named Bill Leu, who is with us here today. His son writes from his home, now in Tokyo, saying: "A half century ago, my father's thoughts were on surviving the attack and winning the war. He could not have envisioned a future where his son would study and work in Japan. But he recognizes that the world has changed, that America's challenges are different. My father's attitude represents that of the United States: Do your duty, and raise the next generation to do its."

I can understand Bill's feelings. I wondered how I'd feel being with you, the veterans of Pearl Harbor—the survivors—on this very special day. And I wondered if I would feel that intense hatred that all of us felt for the enemy 50 years ago. As I thought back to that day of infamy and the loss of friends, I wondered: What will my reaction be when I go back to Pearl Harbor?

Well, let me tell you how I feel. I have no rancor in my heart toward Germany or Japan—none at all. And I hope, in spite of the loss, that you have none in yours. This is no time for recrimination.

World War II is over. It is history. We won. We crushed totalitarianism—and when that was done, we helped our enemies give birth to democracies. We made our enemies our friends . . .

Now, just speaking for one guy, I have no rancor in my heart. I can still see the faces of fallen comrades, and I'll bet you can still see the faces, too . . . But don't you think they're saying 50 years have passed, and we are at peace? Don't you think each one is saying: "I did not die in vain"?

May God bless each of you who sacrificed and served. And may God grant his loving protection to this, the greatest country on the face of the Earth, the United States of America.

Thank you all, and God bless you. Thank you very much.

President Bush gave a powerful speech that day, one that has stuck with me through the years. He words resonated with me and no doubt with many veterans in the audience and those who listened from home and abroad.

Attending that ceremony was hard, but the best thing that happened to me was I was finally able to put aside the wrongs of what happened that day and start to see the best of everything. The fiftieth remembrance provided me with an opportunity to rekindle some friendships with old shipmates and provided the spark for Val and me to return in the coming years for the fifty-fifth (in 1996), sixtieth (in 2001), and sixty-fifth (in 2006). After that, Val and I attended every year we could, which was most years, until 2015.

In the early days of our travels for the December 7 services, there were only a handful of us who went to Hawaii, but in the years that followed, more and more family and friends began accompanying us. Eventually, our travel party numbered in the forties, and we quickly became known as the "Conterage" to the rangers at the park. I may not have said it, but I always appreciated the support I've received from family and friends on the trips to Hawaii. It truly meant a lot to me to have those I care about the most share the experience of being at the memorial on the anniversary of the attack.

In 1996, Val and I moved back to Bend, Oregon, again when I was hired to take care of several properties and developments. We bought a house right next to the Bend Golf Club. The club, which dated back to 1925, was a championship course that hosted the Oregon Open, Northwest Open, Oregon Amateur, PNGA Women's Amateur, PNGA Mid-Amateur, and many more.

In 2001, Val was growing weary of all the moves we had been making, and she wanted to settle down. I had turned eighty and had been on the go since I was eighteen years old. Now, sixty-two years later, I was finally ready to put down some roots.

We began investigating places to live, and a friend of ours from Indian Wells suggested we look at homes in Nevada County, California, which is in the northern part of the state. This gal had a second home in Penn Valley, California, and offered us the use of it for a while so we could check out the area. Well, after the first two days, we were sold.

We eventually decided to live in Grass Valley, which is in the western foothills of the Sierra Nevada mountain range about sixty miles east of Sacramento and eighty-eight miles west of Reno. With a population of a little over ten thousand when we arrived, Grass Valley was a perfect community for us. Not too big, not too small. A good community. Heck, we even found a go-to place for breakfast that we both loved, a little place called the Breakfast Club Café. The owner, Mary Johanson, had the place decked to the hilt in red, white, and blue, giving it an extremely patriotic theme. There were American-flag wallpaper borders, flags on the tables, and Uncle Sam, USA, and "I Love America" wall decorations throughout the entire place. It was incredible. She also had a photograph of one of the more iconic photos from that fateful day. Most people have seen it. The photograph is of two sailors on Ford Island watching the carnage. One of the sailors is seated on the ground, and the other is standing; both are watching an enormous fireball and thick black smoke coming from the airfield and rolling into the sky. Well, I asked Mary about the photograph, and she told me it was of her father and that he was stationed in Hawaii during the attack. I could not believe it. Furthermore, she said her father, Richard Edward Stopp, was a radioman on a PBY. Imagine that!

The Breakfast Club Café instantly became our favorite place to eat, and we usually went there at least two or three times a week. I even started holding Pearl Harbor Survivors meetings there as well. Mary was a great gal. We all hit it off right away. To this day, some twenty years later, she remains one of my best friends.

In 2003, we met Jack and Linda Kennedy, who, like Mary, are close friends to this day. In fact, Mary, Jack, and Linda are so much more than friends; they are family. Jack and Linda had moved into the neighborhood to care for Linda's stepmother, Maggie, who had been diagnosed with terminal cancer. We first met Linda when her mother fell out of her wheelchair, and we went over to help. Later, we invited the Kennedys to dinner. It did not take too long for me to know that we were all going to become fast friends.

Like me, Jack was a Navy man, and Val and Linda struck up an immediate friendship. There were many nights when Jack and I would have a scotch and sometimes a cigar. Linda would have a brandy, and Val would have a glass of wine. They were great people, and we enjoyed their company so much that it was not uncommon to have dinner and drinks with the Kennedys two or three times a week. Linda's mom passed in 2005. It was a hard time, but we were all there for each other, and from that sadness, our friendship grew even stronger.

We had another bump in the road in 2009. I wasn't feeling

very well, so I went to my doctor in Green Valley. After a few tests, the doctor thought that maybe I had a transient ischemic attack (TIA), so I was put in the hospital and underwent more tests. As it turned out, I needed a four-way bypass, so I was sent down to Mercy Hospital in Sacramento. The doctors at Mercy were very reluctant to do the surgery because I was eighty-eight.

I knew I had to have the surgery, so Val and I discussed the pros and cons of having or not having it. We were advised of the risks, and after careful consideration, I said to the doctor, "Let's do this."

The surgery went well, but it ended up being a five-way bypass. The day after surgery, I was alone in my room and had to go to the bathroom. I did not want to bother the nurse, so I sat up and started unhooking my leads. The next thing I knew, bells and alarms started screeching, and five nurses came running into my room. I had no idea it would create such a fuss.

Two days after surgery, my doctor came in to see me and told me that I would probably be there another ten days. He said one of the criteria for my release was that I would have to blow a fifteen hundred on a peak flow meter. I picked it up, looked at it, and said, "This thing?" The doctor said yes, so I took a breath and blew; the little ball went well past three thousand. My doctor looked at me and said, "Lou, you can probably go home in two more days."

Eight weeks after the surgery, I was back out on the golf course.

For the next few years, Val and I lived life to the fullest. We would visit Lindsay and take trips across the United States, stopping to see all kinds of friends and relatives along the way. We made trips to New York, Washington, and even visited Canada a time or two. We were on an incredible journey. Then, in March of 2012, everything changed, and our world came crashing down upon us.

When Val first became sick, we thought she was just hav-ing trouble fighting a lingering cold. She had signs that she was developing a case of pneumonia, so we took her to our doctor, Qing Tang-Oxley, a wonderful physician whom both Val and I adored.

Dr. Tang-Oxley knew right away that Val's illness was more serious than a case of pneumonia, and after she conducted sever-al tests, we received the shocking news that Val had lung cancer. The news hit me like a ton of bricks. I was devastated; while I had been trained to deal with so many types of horrible situa-tions, nothing prepared me for this. By this time, Val and I had been married for forty-five years. She was my true love. She was my entire world. She meant everything to me. As word got out that Val was sick, some people probably did not think I was even reacting to the news that my wife—my lovely, wonderful, beautiful wife—had cancer. I was not, and still am not, a man who wears his emotions on his sleeve. While it is true that I may not have shown too much emotion during Val's sickness, on the inside, I was utterly shattered, but I had to stay strong for Val. My training told me this was one of those things that we had to take head on, and it was something that we had to handle if we were going to overcome and defeat our enemy, which was cancer.

After meeting with several doctors, the decision was made to remove half of Val's left lung. After the surgery, we received more bad news. With the type of cancer she had, chemotherapy was not an option, so she was put on Tarceva, which is prescribed for patients with non-small cell lung cancer (NSCLC) whose cancer has spread to other parts of the body and that has certain types of epidermal growth factor receptor (EGFR) mutations.

In researching the drug, I learned that Tarceva could not be used for an extended time and that the person who was on the medication longest took it for twenty-seven months before pass-ing away. Had Val not had her lung removed, doctors said she would have only lived for another six to eight weeks. Now with part of her lung removed, and by taking Tarceva, doctors extended her life expectancy to twenty-four to thirty months.

We were determined to make the best of the time we had left with one another, and we did just that; we made every day count. As the months passed, Val needed to take more and more medication. I could tell how horrible she felt, but she never complained—not once. She was not well enough to do anything, but she put up a great front whenever company came to visit. I could see in her eyes how much pain she was in, but she never wavered, and anyone coming into our home would have never imagined how sick she was.

For my ninety-first birthday, which was September 13, 2012, Val wrote me my birthday card; I cherish it to this day.

To my dear husband—This year for your 91st birthday, I am writing your card myself.

I want you to know how much you mean to me. You take such good care of me. I know how awful I look—no hair, skinny, sick looking, etc. You help me walk straight instead of staggering all over the place. You take me to all my doctors' appointments and make sure I have enough root beer. In general, you show me in so many ways how much you care.

Sometimes I get a little cranky, maybe because I'm not feeling like my old self, and you just ignore that.

I want you to know how much I appreciate you every day.

I love you very much!!! Happy Birthday.

That birthday card represented everything that Val was to me: loving, humorous, kind, considerate of other people, and the person I am so grateful to have found and am even more grateful to have spent the majority of my life with. As I said ear-lier, she was my world. She was everything to me.

Despite her illness, Val insisted we continue to plan on at-tending the December 7 ceremonies. It was important to her that we be in Hawaii. Attending the Pearl Harbor Remembrance Ceremonies gave both Val and me an opportunity to not only show our respect to those who had lost their lives at Pearl Har-bor all those years ago but to honor a time in history that should never be forgotten.

We made the trip in 2012, 2013, and 2014, and no one was the wiser as to how sick Val was. She always wore a smile, treat-ed everyone she met with dignity and respect, and always asked how everyone's trip was going and if there was anything that she could do to make it more enjoyable.

The National Park Service has some amazing people work-ing for them; their rangers are incredible, and over the years we've had the honor to meet some great ones. Nicole (Nikki) Elledge Brown and Kelsea Larsen have been great to our family, as has Amanda Thompson, who, in 2012, began helping plan and coordinate the Conterage visits every year since. Amanda has arranged private tours, boat transportation to and from the memorial, and coordinated all our media events. She always asked our visitors how they were doing, what exciting things were happening in their lives, and, of course, if there was any-thing she could do for them. There were years when the Con-terage numbers reached into the mid-forties, and Amanda was always there to help make our visit as pleasant and stress free as possible. In some ways, Amanda helped take some of the pres-sure off Val since my wife was the one who usually had to tend to all the arrangements for our family and friends during all our previous trips.

Shortly after returning from the 2014 trip, USS *Arizona*

survivor Joe Langdell passed away. Joe, who was one hundred years old, was a twenty-seven-year-old ensign aboard the USS *Arizona* during the attack on Pearl Harbor. Well, shortly after Joe's passing, I was approached about speaking at his internment, which would be held in conjunction with the December 7 Remembrance Ceremony, so we began to make plans to attend.

We started to see Val slow down significantly in 2015, and soon she needed around-the-clock care. She was getting sicker and sicker, thinner and thinner, and was just so tired. Every day was a struggle, but she still put on a good front. As December 7 of that year neared, I made the decision that I was not going to go. "Don't be ridiculous," Val said. "You have to go. You were given the honor and responsibility of speaking at Joe's internment, so you must go." I went, and Val watched the ceremony on the computer from her bed.

Shortly after I returned home from Hawaii, on December 15, 2015, Dr. Tang-Oxley, along with several other doctors, came by the house and examined Val. When Val first became sick, we were told that if she went on the medication (Tarceva), she would probably live another twenty-four to thirty months; we were now in month fifty-four. We had beaten the odds. However, the time had come to take Val off the medication; it had done what it was meant to do, which was to prolong her life, and we got two more years than we thought were possible.

Dr. Tang-Oxley shared with me that once we took Val off the medication, she would probably not last more than thirty days. The last year had been so difficult. My heart ached so much as I saw what the cancer was doing to my Val. I had to watch her being cared for twenty-four hours a day and admired her so much for the fight she was putting up; it was one of the bravest things I have seen any person do. Val was one hell of a fighter, but the time had come for me to stop being selfish.

Dr. Tang-Oxley explained the situation to Val, who was comfortable with things. She said she wanted to pass at home, and we all respected her decision.

On Tuesday, January 5, 2016, Val said she wanted to have a picture of the two of us. One of the nurses took a picture of us on her cell phone, and the next day, she came back with a framed photograph of Val and me. I sat beside Val and placed the photo on her pillow. About an hour later, she began to go downhill. The evening nurse came by and took my hand. "Lou, we're losing her," she whispered in my ear. My heart sank, and I felt an emptiness come over me. It was only a few seconds later that I realized Val had passed.

We called Dr. Tang-Oxley. She arrived a short while later, examined Val, and confirmed that my sweet, sweet Val had passed. I was so grateful that my children Louann and Jim were present when she passed and that Jack and Linda had come by earlier to say their goodbyes. But even though I was surrounded by family and friends, I had never felt so alone, and at that moment, my heart felt as if it weighed one hundred pounds.

I was grateful Val passed on her terms, at home with family and friends. She would have turned eighty-seven just two days later. We held a recitation of the rosary on Monday, January 18, and a funeral mass on Tuesday, January 19, both at St. Patrick Catholic Church in Grass Valley. It was a beautiful ceremony.

Val left behind her sisters, Lindsay, Marlene, Lynn Ann, and Linda; her brothers, Glenn and Denny; her five children; her grandchildren; great-grandchildren; and many nieces and nephews, all of whom she loved dearly. All were heartbroken, as was I.

When I lost Val, I also lost a part of me. How could I not? We had forty-seven incredible years together. She was my best friend, and she made me a better person. She treated everyone she encountered with love and kindness. I miss her every single day.

About a year or so ago, Dan Martinez, a great friend and the chief historian at the Pearl Harbor National Memorial, called me up and asked if I was going to be buried on the USS *Arizona*. Had I passed before Val, she would have insisted on it; however, I knew on January 5, 2016, where I was going to be buried, and it was next to Val—right where I belong—right where I want to be.

22

WHY REMEMBERING MATTERS

WHILE VAL HAD NOT attended the seventy-fourth anniversary of the attack on Pearl Harbor with me in 2015, she was still with me; she was with me in spirit and on earth. In 2016, however, that was not the case. Val and I had been going to Pearl Harbor on and off since 1991, and except for not having her with me in 2015, I was never without her at any of the remembrance ceremonies. Being in Hawaii for the seventy-fifth anniversary without Val felt awkward, but I also know that she would have insisted that I be there.

The Seventy-Fifth Pearl Harbor Remembrance Ceremony, in 2016, was an extraordinary event. For some Pearl Harbor survivors, it was their first return to the island since the day of the attack; for others, it would be their last. The week was filled with a wide variety of events. The ceremony itself was memorable as more than four thousand people, including hundreds of Pearl Harbor survivors, World War II veterans, and their families gathered at Kilo Pier. The ceremony included a moment of silence, a fighter jet flyover, and wreath presentations just before 8:00 a.m., the same time of day that the Japanese attack took place on December 7, 1941. It was a beautiful ceremony. There were so many events that I cannot recall every one of them, but for the people with the WWII Valor in the Pacific National Monument, and in particular Amanda Thompson, the event was something special.

The week concluded with Garth Brooks and Trisha Yearwood giving a benefit concert for Pacific Historic Parks and dispersing 100 percent of the net proceeds from the performances to four historical organizations that share the mission of preserving the legacy of Pearl Harbor: WWII Valor in the Pacific National Monument (USS *Arizona* Memorial), Pacific Aviation Museum Pearl Harbor, USS *Bowfin Submarine* Museum & Park, and Battleship Missouri Memorial. I even had the good fortune to have my picture taken with them; Val would have loved it. More stars, musicians, and celebrities need to follow the lead of Mr. Brooks and Ms. Yearwood; we need more people like them.

In 2016, there were only five USS *Arizona* survivors remaining: me, Lonnie Cook, Lauren Bruner, Donald Stratton, and Ken Potts.

I went again to the seventy-sixth anniversary, but health issues kept me away from the next one. I returned to Hawaii in 2019 for the seventy-eighth anniversary, but, sadly, I was the only one of the three remaining survivors able to attend as neither Ken Potts nor Don Stratton could be there. It was a somber trip as Lauren Bruner was interned aboard the USS *Arizona* at sunset after a full day of December 7 activities commemorating the attack on Pearl Harbor. I had the honor of speaking at Lauren's services, the last such service that will ever be held aboard the ship.

As of the writing of this book, only Ken Potts and I are still alive. Ken is no longer able to travel, so the responsibility of representing the men of the USS *Arizona* at remembrance ceremonies falls upon my shoulders. COVID-19 will keep me away from the seventy-ninth anniversary of the attack, but if all goes well and God graces me with a few more years on this earth, I intend to return to Hawaii for the eightieth anniversary, when I will be one hundred years of age.

I will, and I must, do whatever I can do each year to honor the sacrifices of those who gave their lives that day and in the war that followed. Although it's never easy for me to remember the devastation of the attack, and it is difficult to stand there on that platform and look at the names of all the shipmates who were killed that day, I hope that the sacrifices made by those men will live on with Americans for generations. However, I fear that our nation might one day forget about them, a privilege not afforded to those who have served and lost their lives in service to our country.

The Day of Infamy, December 7, 1941, must be remembered mainly so that we, the United States of America, will not be so complacent that it could happen again but also for the 2,403 servicemen and -women who lost their lives at Pearl Harbor, the 1,178 who were wounded, and the 1,500,000 who lost their lives or were wounded in the following years.

Finally, I would like to share with you the story of "The Flag," which every American should know and embrace:

I am the flag of the United States of America. My name is old glory. I fly atop the world's tallest buildings. I stand watch in America's halls of justice. I fly majestically over great institutes of learning, and I stand guard with the greatest military power in the world.

Look up and see me! I stand for peace, honor, truth, and justice. I stand for freedom. I am confident and I am arrogant. I am proud. When I am flown with my fellow banners my head is a little higher, my colors a little truer. I bow to no one, period. I am recognized all over the world. I am honored and saluted. I am respected. I am revered. I am loved and I am feared. I have fought every battle of every war for more than 200 years: Gettysburg, Shiloh, Appomattox, San Juan Hill, the trenches of France, the Argonne Forest, Ansio, Rome, the beaches of Normandy, the deserts of Africa, the cane fields of the Philippines, the rice patties and jungles of Guam, Okinawa, Japan, Korea, Vietnam and scores of places long forgotten by all those who were with me. I was there. I led my soldiers. I followed them. I watched over them. They love me.

I was on a small hill in Iwo Jima. I was dirty, battle worn, and tired, but my soldiers cheered me on, and I was proud.

I have been soiled, burned, torn and trampled on the streets—streets of countries I have helped to set free. It does not hurt, for I am invincible. I have been soiled, burned, torn and trampled on the streets of my own country, and when it is by those with whom I have served in battle, it hurts—but I shall overcome for I am strong.

I have slipped the bonds of earth and stood watch over the uncharted new frontiers of space from my vantage point on the moon. I have been a silent witness to all of America's finest hours. But my finest hour comes when I am torn into strips to be used for bandages for my wounded comrades on the field of battle, when I fly at half-mast to honor soldiers, and when I lie in the trembling arms of grieving mother at the graveside of her fallen child. I am proud.

My name is old glory. Long may I wave. Dear God—long may I wave.

People ask me why, at the age of ninety-nine, I have decided to write a book. Well, there are a few reasons.

I wanted to write this book because the history books in our schools do not have enough information about the raid on Pearl Harbor and the events that led up to the attack. Our young people need to know the truth about this subject. We can never let our youth forget the events that took place on December 7, 1941; it cannot become an event forgotten with the passage of time.

I wanted to write this book because I believe young people can benefit from learning about survival and how to survive during times of adversity. We must teach our young people that they should never panic when they find themselves in a bad situation. Take a deep breath, go over all your options in your head, and develop a plan on how to escape your situation. Find a safe place, and in time, the bad situation will pass.

I wanted to write this book because I am a storyteller, and I believe it is essential for our families to know about their family history. Therefore, I wanted to leave a written record that will one day allow my future great-grandchildren and great-great-grand-children to know who I was. I wanted the future generations of Conters to know my stories and know how important the people in my life were.

I wanted to write this book in hopes that my story will be an inspiration to all and a lifesaver to many. My life was just one of the many lives impacted by the horrors of war. There were those of us who were fortunate to survive and lived to come home to our families. We had children, lived our lives, and many of us were blessed to have lived full and happy lives. We were the lucky ones, and we have a responsibility never to forget those who did not survive, those who did not have the opportunity to enjoy their lives.

Finally, I wanted to write this book because I have a responsibility to remember the 1,177 lost members of the USS *Arizona*. In some small way, I also hope that this book will help pay tribute to my lost shipmates and all veterans who have lost their lives in service to their country. Their sacrifices on December 7, 1941, need to be remembered, understood, and honored.

Authors' Closing

In the spring of 2018, we contacted USS *Arizona* survivor Louis Anthony Conter to see if he would allow us to interview him for a documentary film we were producing on the USS *Arizona* band, entitled *A Band to Honor*. Lou graciously agreed to our interview request, and a few weeks later, we were in his Grass Valley, California, home. As the interview began, we quickly realized Lou Conter was no ordinary man, and, in fact, he was someone special. As we progressed through the one-and-a-half-hour interview, Lou not only shared his experiences aboard the USS *Arizona*, but he also talked about his life—a life before the *Arizona* and his life after that fateful day in December of 1941. As you have just read, his story was incredible. When we asked Lou why he had never written a book or agreed to have a book written about him, his response was, "Who in the world would be interested in my story?" Humility is one of the many qualities we have come to love about Lou.

Soon, we will no longer have anyone from America's Great Generation among us. As the stories of valor and sacrifice can no longer be shared by the voices of those with firsthand knowledge of the critical events in our nation's history, and as the men and women who served around the globe and on the home front pass away, it becomes the responsibility of writers and filmmakers to preserve stories such as Lou's for future generations. We must have books or films that document just how incredible these people truly were. We cannot allow their accounts of sacrifice and heroism ever to be forgotten.

Having the opportunity to get to know Lou Conter, his family, and his friends has been a remarkable experience. We are grateful they welcomed us into their lives and into their family. It was an honor to work on this project with Lou. We cherish each moment we have had with him and will cherish each moment we will have with him in the future. What an incredible man—what a remarkable story.

We want to thank the following people for their support in this project: Randall Bennett, Jeanne and Ed Bonner, Harold L. Brown, Todd Bull, Lee Chambers, Phillip Clark, Jim and Kay Coffey, Linda Wood Colson, Martin Cooperman, Stan Cromlish, Ery De Jong, Scott Denham, Carlo Essagian, Thomas W. Hanna, Carol Hillerson, Ken Hokanson, Brenda and Michael C. Humphrey, Philip M. T. Jacques, Cary Jamison, Donald Johnson, Terry Kaminsky, Jane E. O. Keller, Keri Taylor Hayes, Jonathan Kennedy, Brian H. Leahy, Frederick Linden, Jason Lor, Christina May, Victoria Mccurry, Jack McLaughlin, Teddie and Bill Messier, Rebecca R. Meyer, Ron Miner, Joanne and Greg Piper and family, Kevin Scoggin, Megan Spindler, Loretta and Mike Sweeney, and Erik S. Taylor. Without their generosity, Lou's story may well have slipped into history without ever being recorded, which would have been tragic.

We would also like to thank Ed Bonner for his inspiring introduction. Ed, like Lou, is a humble man and a man of honor; maybe that's one reason why he and Lou have such a strong friendship. Like Lou, Ed Bonner served his country, not in the military but as a member of the Placer County Sheriff's Office in California, where he spent forty-three years with his department, with twenty-two of those years as its top peace officer.

Lastly, we want to give a very special thank-you to Mary Andrew Johanson. For almost a year, Mary was our go-to person when it came to getting information to and from Lou. Mary and Lou's friendship has allowed her to get answers to questions that only a trusted friend could have gotten. It was a tough road at times, but Mary was always there for us to do whatever she could to help bring this book to fruition. She is a wonderful lady, and we love her dearly.

—Annette and Warren Hull, coauthors

BIBLIOGRAPHY

Academy of Achievement. (2020, June 16). *Admiral James B. Stockdale, USN*. Retrieved from Academy of Achievement: https://bit.ly/2VY3h6A

Admiral James B. Stockdale, USN. (2020, June 16). Retrieved from Academy of Achievement: https://bit.ly/33YdXq3

American Forces Press Service. (2013, February 12). *Operation Homecoming for Vietnam POWs marks 40 years*. Retrieved from US Air Force: https://bit.ly/3qI4jSk

Arizona Memorial Museum Association. (2005, July 17). USS *Arizona Memorial—Creating the Memorial*. Retrieved from Arizona Memorial Museum Association: https://bit.ly/3m2SH-FV

Arizona Republic. (2014, December 30). *Why Arizona Banned Booze 100 Years Ago*. Retrieved from AZ Central: https://bit.ly/2LiuHBP

Assembly. (2002, September). Charles Maze Simpson, III. *Assembly, XLIX*(1), 177–178. Retrieved June 20, 2020, from https://cutt.ly/3hTcBZi

Bailey, B., & Farber, D. (1992). *Hotel Street: Prostitution and the Politics of War*. Retrieved from Duke University Press: https://cutt.ly/FhTc973

Bank, A. (1986). *From OSS to Green Berets: The Birth of Special Forces.* Novato, CA: Presidio Press.

Bank, A. (1995, June 25). (D. J. Fischer, Interviewer). Fort Bragg, NC: USASOC Archives.

Bejar, H. (2007). *It's Not About the Coffee.* New York: Penguin Group.

Boyne, W. J. (2002). *Air Warfare: An International Encyclopedia* (Vols. 1, A–L). Santa Barbara, CA: ABC-CLIO, Inc. Retrieved June 16, 2020

Brisco, C. H. (2006). *Major Herbert R. Brucker, SF Pioneer.* Retrieved from Office of the Command Histori: https://cutt.ly/BhTc7bp

Bryan, III, J. (1952). *Admiral Halsey's Story.* Retrieved from University of Chicago: https://cutt.ly/9hTvrz1

Burke, D. (2005, October 31). *Looking 4.* Retrieved from The 379th Bomb Group Archives: https://cutt.ly/FhTvie3

Butler, H. D. (2007, November 18). *Capt. William R. Whorton Knows True Meaning of Service.* Retrieved from The Gadsden Times: https://cutt.ly/YhTvpR1

Carlson, L. H. (2002). *Remembered Prisoners of a Forgotten War: An Oral History of the Korean War POWs.* New York: St. Martin's Press.

Carson, R. (1962). *Silent Spring.* New York: Houghton Mifflin Company.

Chin, C. P. (2020, May 16). *World War II Database.* Retrieved from Line Crossing Ceremony: https://ww2db.com/other.php?other_id=17

City of Tustin, California. (2020, June 16). *Tustin Hangars.* Retrieved from City of Tustin, California: https://cutt.ly/ghTvfKF

Clancey, P. (2020, May 2). *Hyper War.* Retrieved from Office of Strategic Services (OSS) organization and functions: https://cutt.ly/ahTvhXF

CQ Researcher. (1943, November 30). *Disposal of Surplus War Materials*. Retrieved from CQ Researcher: https://cutt.ly/ThTvloP

Crocker, M. (2002). *Black Cats and Dumbos: WW II's Fighting PBYs*. Huntington Beach, CA: Crocker Media Expressions.

Daland, T. (2011, February 9). *The Military Code of Conduct: A Brief History*. Retrieved June 16, 2020, from Kunsan Air Base: https://cutt.ly/2hTvbDS

Denny, R., & Righter, W. H. (2012, January 12). *The Radioplane Target Drone*. Retrieved from Monash University. URL no longer available.

Department of Defense. (2018, February 9). *Department of Defense Executive Agent Responsibilities of the Secretary of the Army*. Retrieved from Army Publishing Directorate: https://cutt.ly/lhTvGNk

Doran, A. R., Hoyt, G. B., Lauby-Hiller, M. D., & Morgan III, C. A. (2006). Survival, Evasion, Resistance, and Escape (SERE) Training: Preparing Military Members for the Demands of Captivity. *American Psychological Association*, 306–330.

Eisenhower, D. (1955, August 17). *Executive Order 10631—Code of Conduct for Members of the Armed Forces of the United States*. Retrieved from National Archives: https://cutt.ly/8hTvKNC

Fawcett, D. (2015). *The Brothels of Chinatown*. Retrieved from Honolulu Civil Beat: https://cutt.ly/JhTvV3F

Finlayson, K. (2006). *Colonel Aaron Bank—1902–2004*. Retrieved from Office of the Command Historian: https://cutt.ly/vhTv2jt

Fleet Marine Force Reconnaissance. (2020, July 4). *1st Force Reconnaissance Company*. Retrieved from Military: https://cutt.ly/yhTv71Z

Foley, J. (2019, March 4). Retired Brigadier General, US Army—CEO/President of the Servant Leadership Institute. (W. Hull, Interviewer)

Forcerecon. (2017, August). *Colonel Bruce F. Meyers—FRA #7—Dies at Age 91*. Retrieved from Force Recon Association—US Marine Corp: https://cutt.ly/NhTbqos

Giangreco, D. M. (2009). *Hell to Pay: Operation Downfall and the Invasion of Japan*. Annapolis, MD: Naval Institute Press. Retrieved from https://cutt.ly/ahTbePv

Gibson, J. (2020, June 16). *Rear Admiral Isaac Campbell Kidd*. Retrieved from Silent Heroes: https://cutt.ly/5hTbt4n

Gowdy, J. D. (1996). *The Institute for American Liberty*. Retrieved from Seven Principles of Liberty: http://www.liberty1.org/seven.htm

Green, R. (2018, July 26). *OSS Plank Holder and Special Operations Legend Laid to Rest at Arlington*. Retrieved from United States Special Operations Command: https://cutt.ly/whTb-f9q

Greenspan, J. (2019, February 13). *George H. W. Bush's Role in WWII Was among the Most Dangerous*. Retrieved from History: https://cutt.ly/lhTbj4x

Haas, M. (2001). *In the Devil's Shadow: UN Special Operations during the Korean War*. Annapolis, MD: Naval Institute.

Harrington, J., & Suneson, G. (2019, June 13). *What Were the 13 Most Expensive Wars in U.S. History?* Retrieved from USA Today: https://cutt.ly/JhTbx0X

Heinze, E. A. (2009). *Waging Humanitarian War*. New York: State University of New York, Albany.

History.com Editors. (2020, July 17). *Korean War*. Retrieved from History: https://cutt.ly/2hTbm2N

IBP USA. (2016). *United States Special Operation Forces Handbook* (Vol. 3). Washington, DC: International Business Publications.

Kennedy, J. F. (1956). *Profiles in Courage*. New York: Harper and Brothers.

Klinger, B. (2016, May 31). *The Atomic Bomb Averted Even Larger Tragedies*. Retrieved from The Heritage Foundation: https://cutt.ly/hhTbRsc

Legacy. (2015, January 18). *Gene Taft*. Retrieved from Legacy: https://cutt.ly/chTbYGx

Lowry, T. S. (1989). *Valor*. New York, NY: Berkeley Books.

Marolda, E. J. (2020, June 19). *The U.S. Navy in the Cold War Era, 1945–1991*. Retrieved from Naval History and Heritage Command: https://cutt.ly/mhTbOnP

Mersky, P. B. (1983). *U.S. Marine Corps Aviation: 1912 to the Present*. Annapollis, MD: The Nautical and Aviation Publishing Company of America.

Meyers, B. F. (2001). *Fortune Favors the Brave: The Story of First Force Recon*. Annapolis: Naval Institute.

Moore, D. (2013, March 25). *Veteran United*. Retrieved from Pollywog or Shellback: The Navy's Line Crossing Ceremony Revealed: https://cutt.ly/ihTbSX0

National Park Service—Department of the Interior. (2004, July). *Historic American Buildings Survey*. Retrieved from Library of Congress: https://cutt.ly/dhTbGob

Naval History and Heritage Command. (2020). *Naval Air Station Pensacola, Florida*. Retrieved from Naval History and Heritage Command: https://cutt.ly/2hTbLRz

Naval History and Heritage Command. (2020, June 16). *William Lowndes Calhoun*. Retrieved from Naval History and Heritage Command: https://cutt.ly/rhTbXZn

Office of Strategic Services (OSS) Organization and Functions. (1945, June). Retrieved June 16, 2020, from Ibiblio: https://cutt.ly/jhTbNNU

Pelley, R. (2020, May 2). *Mosla and Benzin*. Retrieved from Gander Airport Historical Society: https://cutt.ly/0hTb0jt

Public Affairs—Central Intelligence Agency. (2008, March 15). *The Office of Strategic Services: America's First Intelligence Agency*.

Retrieved June 16, 2020, from Central Intelligence Agency: https://cutt.ly/UhTb3ke

Rawicz, S. (1956). *The Long Walk: The True Story of a Trek to Freedom.* New York, NY: Harper Books.

Roberts, M. D. (2000). *Dictionary of American Naval Aviation Squadrons* (Vol. 2). Washington, DC: Naval Historical Center, Department of the Navy. Retrieved June 16, 2020

Rohn, A. (2014, January 22). *The Vietnam War.* Retrieved from https://thevietnamwar.info/how-much-vietnam-war-cost/: https://thevietnamwar.info/how-much-vietnam-war-cost/

Salty Old Dog School. (2020, February 19). *Navy Crow.* Retrieved from Navy Crow: https://cutt.ly/rhTnrIC

San Francisco Chronicle. (1999, March 25). *Roy Lee Johnson.* Retrieved from San Francisco Chronicle: https://cutt.ly/yhTnuQo

Sederberg, A. (1967, April 18). Financial Federation President Runs Into Shareholders' Fire. *Los Angeles Times*, 43. Los Angeles, CA: Los Angeles Times. Retrieved June 30, 2020, from https://cutt.ly/qhTnoOM

Smith, H. M. (2002, October 31). NASA Johnson Space Center Oral History Project. (R. Wright, Interviewer) Retrieved from https://cutt.ly/AhTnaFg

Smithsonian National Air and Space Museum. (2020). *Consolidated PBY-5 Catalina.* Retrieved from Smithsonian National Air and Space Museum: https://cutt.ly/GhTngWZ

SwimSwam. (2018, September 19). *Teaching America's WWII Navy Fighter Pilots to Swim.* Retrieved from SwimSwam: https://cutt.ly/0hTnjUb

The Central Intelligence Agency. (2020, July 24). *History of the CIA.* Retrieved from Central Intelligence Agency: https://www.cia.gov/about-cia/history-of-the-cia

The Cottage Grove Sentinel. (2013, February 6). *Lt. Col. John*

Arthur Kupsick. Retrieved from The Cottage Grove Sentinel: https://cutt.ly/7hTnzoa

The Florida Historical Society. (2020). *The Florida Historical Society*. Retrieved from Naval Air Station Pensacola: https://cutt.ly/BhTnc4K

The Greater Northwest Football Association. (2020). USS *Arizona*. Retrieved May 2, 2020, from The Greater Northwest Football Association: https://cutt.ly/WhTnnnT

The Hall of Valor Project. (2020, March 18). *Herman Hansen*. Retrieved from The Hall of Valor Project: https://cutt.ly/shTnQCJ

The Hall of Valor Project. (2020, March 3). *John W. Clapper*. Retrieved from The Hall of Valor Project: https://valor.militarytimes.com/hero/502833

The Hall of Valor Project. (2020, July 17). *Lawrence W. Smith*. Retrieved from The Hall of Valor Project: https://valor.militarytimes.com/hero/44719

The Hall of Valor Project. (2020, July 17). *Leon Newby Utter*. Retrieved from The Hall of Valor Project: https://valor.militarytimes.com/hero/39699

The Office of the Chief of Naval Operations. (1958). Naval Aviation in Review. *Naval Aviation In Review*.

The US Army OCS Alumni Association. (2020, July 4). *Joseph J. Koontz*. Retrieved from The US Army OCS Alumni Association : https://ocsalumni.org/at_biz_dir/joseph-j-koontz/

The West Point Connection. (1990, September). *15352 Simpson, Charles M*. Retrieved from The West Point Connection: https://www.west-point.org/users/usma1946/15352/

Tip of the Spear. (2008, June). *Tip of the Spear*. Retrieved from United States Special Operations Command: https://cutt.ly/DhTnTFR

Trojan, D. (2020, June 16). *They Stood Watch . . . The Story of Patrol Squadron Eleven at NAS Kaneohe Bay*. Retrieved from

Japanese Aircraft, Ships, and Historical Research: https://cutt.ly/VhTnIi0

Trueman, C. N. (2015, March 25). *History Learning Site*. Retrieved from John F. Kennedy and Vietnam: https://cutt.ly/DhTnPKJ

US Army. (2011, April). *Distinguished Member of the Special Forces Regiment*. Retrieved from United States Army Special Operations Command: https://cutt.ly/mhTnS9Q

US Constitution. (2015). *U.S. Constitution*. Retrieved March 17, 2019, from Constitutional Topic: Checks and Balances: https://www.usconstitution.net/consttop_cnb.html

USNA Virtual Memorial Hall. (2020, May 16). *Franklin Van Valkenburgh, Captain, USN*. Retrieved from USNA Virtual Memorial Hall: https://cutt.ly/2hTnGQK

US Navy. (2020, June 16). *Historic California Posts, Camps, Stations and Airfields—Naval Hospital, San Diego Unit 6 (Rancho Santa Fe)*. Retrieved from Military Museum: http://www.militarymuseum.org/NavHospSD6.html

US Navy Department. (1947). *Building the Navy's Bases in World War II*. Washington, DC: United States Government Printing Office.

USSArizona.org. (2015, November 22). *Donald Alexander Graham*. Retrieved from USSArizona.org: https://cutt.ly/dhTnZec

Wikipedia. (2020, July 17). *Battle of Masan*. Retrieved from Wikipedia: https://en.wikipedia.org/wiki/Battle_of_Masan

Wikipedia. (2020, April 24). *Harold C. Train*. Retrieved from Wikipedia: https://en.wikipedia.org/wiki/Harold_C._Train

Wilkinson, S. (2019, August 31). *Cat Tales: The Story of World War II's PBY Flying Boat*. Retrieved from Navy Times: https://cutt.ly/ZhTnVBX

Williamsom, J., Jones, B. T., Myers, H. P., Marshall, G. G., & Williamsom, J. P. (2020, July 24). *USAFSS to AF ISR Agency,*

1948–2009: A Brief History of the AF ISR Agency and Its Predecessor Organizations. Retrieved July 24, 2020, from AF ISR Agency History Office: https://cutt.ly/WhTn1s8

Windeler, R. (1978). *Films of Shirley Temple.* New York: Mc-Graw-Hill.

Wolk, H. S. (1987). The Other Founding Father. *Air Force Magazine, 70*(9). Retrieved May 30, 2020

Zimmerman, D. J. (2012, June 11). *10th Special Forces Group.* Retrieved from Defense Media Netword: https://cutt.ly/YhTn2Cq

Made in United States
Troutdale, OR
04/02/2024

18886407R00145